MW00461534

CHILL OUT, BRO

HOW TO FREAK OUT LESS, ATTACK ANXIETY, CALM WORRY, & REWIRE YOUR BRAIN FOR RELIEF FROM PANIC, STRESS, & ANXIOUS NEGATIVE THOUGHTS

REESE OWEN

CONTENTS

© Copyright 2020 by Reese Owen - All rights reserved.

The following book is reproduced below with the goal of providing information that is as accurate and reliable as possible. Regardless, purchasing this eBook can be seen as consent to the fact that both the publisher and the author of this book are in no way experts on the topics discussed within and that any recommendations or suggestions that are made herein are for entertainment purposes only. Professionals should be consulted as needed prior to undertaking any of the action endorsed herein.

This declaration is deemed fair and valid by both the American Bar Association and the Committee of Publishers Association and is legally binding throughout the United States.

Furthermore, the transmission, duplication or reproduction of any of the following work including specific information will be considered an illegal act irrespective of if it is done electronically or in print. This extends to creating a secondary or tertiary copy of the work or a recorded copy and is only allowed with express written consent from the Publisher. All additional rights reserved.

The information in the following pages is broadly considered to be a truthful and accurate account of facts, and as such any inattention, use or misuse of the information in question by the reader will render any resulting actions solely under their purview. There are no scenarios in which the publisher or the original author of this work can be in any fashion deemed liable for any hardship or damages that may befall them after undertaking information described herein.

Additionally, the information in the following pages is intended only for informational purposes and should thus be thought of as universal. As befitting its nature, it is presented without assurance regarding its prolonged validity or interim quality. Trademarks that are mentioned are done without written consent and can in no way be considered an endorsement from the trademark holder.

IF YOU NEED MORE HELP...

While anxiety is very common and relatively easy to manage and improve for most, in the most severe cases, sometimes further professional help is needed. If that turns out to be the case for you, don't hesitate to reach out to a doctor, mental health professional, or start with contacting one of the many free, 24-hour confidential anxiety or mental illness helplines where they can further assist you and point you in the right direction towards what you need. The phone number varies based on organizations in your region or country, but contact information is very readily available via internet search. Google's got your back.

And so do I.

Wishing you the best on your journey to mental health and well-being.

-Reese

ALL BOOKS BY YOURS TRULY

I'm a very busy, very prolific writer.

In fact, I have so many books about getting your ish together and living your best life, that I have a website:

ReeseOwenBooks.com

Look, Ma, I made it!

Check out my other ebooks, paperback books, and audiobooks available on Amazon and Audible.

B*TCH DON'T KILL MY VIBE:

How To Stop Worrying, End Negative Thinking, Cultivate Positive Thoughts, And Start Living Your Best Life

JUST DO THE DAMN THING:

How To Sit Your @ss Down Long Enough To Exert Willpower, Develop Self Discipline, Stop Procrastinating, Increase Productivity, And Get Sh!t Done

MAKE YOUR BRAIN YOUR B*TCH:

Mental Toughness Secrets To Rewire Your Mindset To Be Resilient And Relentless, Have Self Confidence In Everything You Do, And Become The Badass You Truly Are

INTRODUCTION

Let's talk a little bit about anxiety, shall we?

Anxiety is a real ~~bitch~~ treat, am I right? Ok, good talk.

Ok, seriously...

Anxiety is *seriously* a bitch.

One moment things are perfectly normal, then the next, things are still perfectly normal...for everyone else but you. It suddenly hits you: this gut-wrenching feeling that something is going to go terribly wrong—and before you know it, the worrying sets in. Everyone says that it will be fine or that you just need to think positive, but in your brain, you're telling them where they can take that advice and shove it because—let's be honest—you do not *feel* fine, do you? No, you feel like something is horribly wrong, and you cannot seem to help that feeling nor identify why you're feeling it.

All you know is that your brain is telling you that it was doomsday 5 minutes ago and that you're on borrowed time. Borrowed time for what? Who knows? Still, you cannot shake the feeling that something bad is going to happen. Whatever it is, it's not going to work out. Not for you anyway. For everyone else, sure, but not for you. There you go again—worrying about things that are unknown as if they're known, worrying about things that are uncertain as if they're certain, worrying about things that have not happened as if they have happened, worrying about things that are untrue as if they are true, and worrying about what other people think as if it matters.

And since this whole cycle seems to happen in your life every eight and a half minutes, you're starting to feel like a slave to your anxiety.

And it's getting kind of old.

Let's take a look into the world of my friend Jason for a minute to get a deeper feel for what anxiety is like for him.

Jason is a 25-year-old man (or boy, as some may argue), living with two roommates and attending a regular 9-to-5 office job at a bank, where he was hired right out of college. Jason has a mountain of student loan debt to pay off, an on-again-off-again girlfriend, and a cat whose favorite hobby is barfing all over his clean work clothes just minutes before he needs to leave for work.

Jason got a cat because somewhere along the way, a blog told him that he needed a therapy animal to keep him company, make him feel calm, and increase his quality of life. But so far Jason's therapy animal only causes him to need more therapy, as the only thing it loves to do more than vomiting on his work clothes is using its scratching post—I'm sorry, using Jason's brand new ergonomic desk chair he just skipped a month's student loan payment to buy for $400, as a scratching post. Jason is starting to think that his therapy cat wasn't properly trained or vetted. Jason is starting to think that he should have gotten a therapy goldfish. Or maybe just therapy.

But all in all (minus the sadistic cat), Jason has a pretty standard lifestyle for someone his age…a somewhat steady job, a somewhat steady paycheck, and a somewhat steady relationship. Nothing feels like it's the best it could possibly be, but he doesn't really have it in him to push for something better.

He knows he should probably apply for a better job, but he doesn't feel qualified, so he can't seem to get himself to sit down in that $400 ~~cat scratching post~~ ergonomic chair long enough to apply. And the thought of going in to a job interview makes him feel about as physically sick as the thought of him having "the talk" with his on-again off-again girlfriend about their obviously failing relationship. What if he breaks up with her? And dies. Then he would officially die alone.

Maybe he should go out with friends to take his mind off of everything, but wait—he doesn't have any friends, because he always skips those happy hour socials after work. What if they don't like his jokes? What if they don't like his cowlick? Instead of risking someone not liking his jokes or cowlick, better to not have friends. At least that's how Jason sees it. And the few acquaintances he does know from college he doesn't talk to anymore because they're doing better in life than he is and they're going to want a life update.

What will he say? He *still* has a sadistic cat and an almost equally sadistic girlfriend and that low level job that barely pays him enough to cover minimum payments on that mountain of student loan debt? Oh wait—that's not an update, that's exactly the same thing he was doing last year. And the year before that. And the year before that. He wants to take a hot shower to calm down, but his water heater doesn't work, and he doesn't want to bug the landlord about it because it will call attention to the fact that he hasn't paid his portion of the rent yet. And why has he not paid his portion of the rent, but paid for a $400 chair and kitty litter for the devil cat? Thanks a lot for asking. Now he's stressed that his poor financial decisions are going to drive him to a permanent life of destitution and squalor.

Everything is overwhelming, dizzying, and he feels trapped, which makes him feel stressed. Stress turns into worry. Worry turns into fear. Fear turns into anxiety. Anxiety turns into panic. Panic turns into paralysis. He can't think. He can't breathe. He can't sleep. And half the time, all he wants to do is sleep. Jason is reasonably intelligent and has the capability to do whatever he wants to do, but he just can't seem to do it. He cannot seem to shake the feeling that everything in his life is horribly wrong and getting progressively worse, and something bad is going to happen any minute—no, scratch that—*every* minute.

See, on a day-to-day basis, Jason experiences anxiety for about 960 minutes straight. That's right—from the moment he opens his eyes in the morning until the moment he closes them at night—that is, *if* he can close them at night with all that worrying in this mind. In short, Jason feels like complete crap 24/7. He cannot put his finger on exactly when it started, but at some point between being born and getting to this point in his life 25 years later, Jason started to feel like someone had attached a permanent clamp-on vise around his chest that they tighten at their will whenever they sense that Jason's too close to getting happy or mentally at ease.

Sometimes, he has soul-crushing pressure weighing down on his chest, coupled with a pounding, dizzying headache. Other times, it's not quite so disturbing. But it is always very clearly present. Jason knows that he has a pretty standard life and he even sometimes believes that cheesy t-shirt his mom sent him that says his future's so bright he needs shades. However, he can't seem to stop the constant barrage of thoughts in his head about the presentation he has to do at work, the bills he has to pay, the fight with his girlfriend he should probably break up with anyway, and just the fact that people are looking at him and judging him *all* the time...so he thinks. Jason has tried for years to get his anxiety under control, yet he still feels like a complete nutcase every time he wakes up and realizes that he's not doing too hot at this whole life thing.

And then there's Lindsey. She's a 28-year-old Brand Strategist at a top marketing agency. She goes nuts when things don't go according to plan...to her ten year plan. Plus, she's dating a younger guy who spends $400 on office furniture. He has a $400 chair, yet still lives with two other roommates. She's afraid that kind of fiscal irresponsibility will rub off on her. Then she'll succumb to financial ruin, letting her parents and everybody down. She's afraid she's hit a glass ceiling at her current job, so she's looking for another one. Last week, she stopped by her boyfriend's house on the way to a big interview. And his cat threw up all over her. That wasn't on the ten year plan.

That's the thing about anxiety. It can show up in our lives in ways that don't always feel like anxiety. It may just feel like general life dysfunction or pessimism. But it often involves irrational feelings and irrational behavior in response to irrational evaluations of situations. You know how crazy it is. And you know that a lot of it is rooted in irrational fear. But you still feel it anyway because it swoops in and takes control over you, leaving you as a writhing ball of sweat.

Anxiety sometimes makes zero sense, yet it can completely take you out if you are not fully aware of what is going on with you or why, and you have no idea of what to do to mitigate it. The chances are that if you are reading this book, you feel just like Jason or Lindsey do—crazy, distraught, out of control, maybe a little hopeless, and probably pretty annoyed that you cannot seem to get a grip on life. You're living your life at the mercy of whenever your next anxiety attack, panic attack, worry spiral, fear outbreak, or general freak out decides to strike again.

Maybe you've read a million and one books about mindfulness and meditation and have driven your anxiety up even higher trying to get it right. Or maybe you have read none because you're scared of becoming "one of *those* people." Or maybe this is the first book you are reading because you are ready for your no-bullshit answer to healing this chaos in your brain. Either way, you have come to the right place to finally get the answers on why your brain behaves like this and how to implement some effective strategies so that you can knock it off already.

Anxiety is like shit. It stinks. It doesn't serve you in any way. It's better out than in. And the signs and smells that you have it on you can be embarrassing. Yet, somehow, you manage to convince yourself that you have to keep walking around with it because there is nowhere else to put it. Maybe you have even grown so used to it that you no longer smell just how pungent and horrible the odor really is because it's been with you for so long. That's right. You've gone nose blind to your own anxious shit.

The truth is: anxiety is just a part of your baggage that you have convinced yourself that you have to keep carrying. At some point, you have trained yourself not only to carry this shit baggage, but to open it up and sit in it every time a trigger arises in your life that causes you to feel like something bad is about to happen. And unfortunately for you, that's about every five seconds. In your logical mind, you may know that there's another solution, a better way, but your emotional mind has grown so used to making a beeline straight for anxiety that you have an incredibly challenging time allowing yourself to move into a more logical and healthy approach to handling your thoughts and keeping them from spiraling.

So you keep digging back into your baggage full of poop and covering yourself in the foul odor of life repellant, which ensures that everything that is good about life remains at an arms' length away...maybe even a little further than that considering the poop stench. And it's starting to feel just as crazy as it sounds to do such a thing and hold yourself back in such a seemingly controllable way. Yet you keep on doing it.

At this point, your anxiety may be showing up in your life in some pretty crazy ways. You may feel it when you wake up in the morning and realize that you have to go to a job you hate with a boss you're afraid to speak up to, so you begin to feel tense and sweaty. You might notice it when you are on the subway and some strange man side eyes you from three seats over, and you start wondering if you have evidence of this morning's maple bacon donut still around your mouth, or if he is going to steal your wallet and club you with that cane he's using to pretend to be handicapped.

Maybe when you are sitting at home alone, you feel soul-crushing anxiety that stems from thinking you are unworthy of true friends or true love, and from the fear to go out and meet people at the risk of rejection. Or maybe for you it happens when you are out at social events with your friends or your lover, and it feels like all of the air in the room is being used up by everyone else. In fact, you may even find yourself feeling chronically agitated, angry, or aggressive because of how anxious you are, and you may not even realize that it is your anxiety that is causing you to feel like you might be the next Connor McGregor.

Anxiety is probably creeping up in your life in ways that extend even further than what you assume to be possible. She can be a sneaky, tip-toeing little biotch that can pop out from around the corner out of nowhere. You may find that as you work through this book, you discover that you are way more anxious than you thought you were and that it's a good thing you found yourself here sorting your stuff out.

The National Alliance on Mental Illness states that nearly 1 in 5 adults in the US has some form of anxiety. So as we can see, anxiety is common, but ironically, most people with anxiety seem to think they're the only ones, so they suffer in silence, and only 36.9% of Americans with anxiety get treatment. If we extrapolate that to a worldwide scale, 300 million people have some form of anxiety disorder according to the World Health Organization.

And then there's the people who don't think they have it at all.

Still think you don't have anxiety? Still think I'm not talking about you—nail biting, house a complete mess, perpetual eye twitch, snoozes 9 times to avoid getting out of bed to face the day—*you*? Still think your friend accidentally ordered this book on Amazon and *accidentally* typed your name and shipping address in the checkout page? Still think this book ending up in your hands isn't a wink-wink nudge-nudge to give you a wake-up call?

I guess I can say that in a way, I get it. I mean, after all, the word "anxiety" sounds so formal, and having to take possession of it feels so permanent. "Anxiety" is so ubiquitous and overused, yet so serious at the same time. The weight of the word carries with it the definiteness of a diagnosis and the shame of having...an issue...a real live issue. The term can be off-putting for some...my former self included. So like many people, I myself denied that I even had anxiety.

Oh no I don't have anxiety, I'm just running through my life scared shitless that something is going to go wrong, but I don't have anxiety.

I don't have anxiety, I'm just incessantly worried to death that I'm going to lose everything and everyone that I love, and I'm constantly sick to my stomach because of it.

Oh, I don't have anxiety, I'm just so stressed out that I can't think straight, and have perpetual migraines that keep me up at night.

For some, the word carries a severe, even painful connotation. But for all, the goal is to just get the heck over it so we can get on with our lives. Getting over anxiety can be fun. I can guarantee getting over it is more fun than being plagued by it. So let's poke a little fun at this boogeyman who lives inside all of us to some degree and let's kill it once and for all. Or at least long enough to buy us time to think clearly enough to make our next life decision.

If you don't want to be caught with a book about anxiety, fine.

Because this is really a book about fear. Because isn't that what anxiety really is? Fear of something bad happening.

Actually this is a book about stress...since anxiety is really just stressing over the fear of something bad happening.

No, this is a book about worry...worrying about the worst possible outcome for any and every situation that happens in your life, and worrying that no matter what happens, you won't be able to handle it.

Whether you call it anxiety, stress, or worry, at the root, they are all fear, and they all have the same negative mental, emotional, and physical consequences to you and your life. And the easiest way to wrap them all up in one pretty little asshole bow is to call it anxiety. So in this book, I'm talking about anxiety and its many cousins.

Anxiety comes in many forms, varying levels of severity, and it also has many related root causes. So while I'll often use the word "anxiety," you can substitute that word for stress, fear, or worry. And while we often say that people "have" anxiety, it doesn't have to be a permanent part of who you are. It can just be something that you temporarily experience until you learn to get a handle on it.

Anxiety is physical. It's mental. It's emotional. There are parts of it that are within your control, and there are parts of it that make you feel like you're possessed and have absolutely no say in what's going on with you and how you react to things. To talk about anxiety without addressing it from all of these angles and providing solutions from all of these angles, is to not really talk about anxiety. And that's why I've put this book together the way that I did.

It is divided into five easily digestible, stress-free parts. If you're the antsy type, try not to skip around, but here's an overview of how this book is laid out so you know what to expect:

Part 1 is all about going over a few common types of anxiety, some of the scientific reasons behind it, why it can feel so bad, and how it can get out of hand without you realizing it. This part will help you validate yourself and your experience and help you to stop feeling like something's wrong with you every time "just being positive" doesn't seem to cut it.

Part 2 is about getting more acquainted with the problem —more specifically getting acquainted with *your* problem. Each chapter of Part 2 is dedicated to a different cause of anxiety that is within your control, and each chapter ends with some exploratory questions designed to help you get to the root causes of your anxiety so you can start to notice areas where you can make changes. In this part of the book, self-awareness comes into play so that you can start seeing where you are tripping up, not just hoping to hold on tight for dear life until each attack is over, praying to get to the other side as fast as possible.

Part 3 is dedicated to different ways you can make changes to your behavior, practices, and mindset to bring calm to anxious moments.

Part 4 covers three popular and proven methods that therapists use to treat anxiety. It is meant to expose you to the opportunity to find ways to implement these methods, in whole or in part, into your life if you so choose or feel the need.

Part 5 is about tactics to ease the anxious beast that are based on mental habits and shifts that work best when implemented consistently over the long term.

So that's it. It doesn't sound like a lot when you summarize it in a few sentences, but it can feel like a lot more when you're actually reading through it and taking action on it. But take your time. You don't want to get stressed and anxious about the book that's supposed to help you be less stressed and anxious.

Here's the good news about all this. There is something you can do. It is not hopeless. *You* are not hopeless. Ever heard of neuroplasticity? It essentially means that your brain can be rewired with new information and that with time and repetition, it will slowly eliminate any outdated information that is no longer serving it. So, if you want to eliminate anxiety, you simply need to use better tools that effectively serve your brain and give you the ability to manage your anxiety in a healthier way. And for the tools, you have come to the right place.

There are very real, very simple, and very effective practices you can implement that can change your brain, change your behavior, and change your life. All you need to do is show up and read the book (the whole book) and follow the prompts. That means do what I tell you to do. The only way these tactics don't work is if you don't do them. I promise, if you take to heart what is discussed in Part 2 of this book, and take action on what is discussed in Parts 3, 4, and 5 you can and will feel like a normal human again. You're going to be able to understand why your brain is bugging out, and start feeding it new information and resources that support it in responding in a healthy and functional way so it can chill out and stop always holding you on the edge of a psychotic episode that never seems to happen...most of the time.

But this process will require you to be open to looking inside you for things that are not always pretty, be open to change, and it will require that you take accountability and responsibility, recognizing that you are the one in control. If you don't take personal responsibility and you don't take action, I can guarantee you that nothing will change.

So get excited. The times of you being a reckless recluse with no real friends, tiny little chewed up nails, and a chronic shiver that will not seem to go away are soon coming to an end. Instead of living like you constantly think a piano is going to fall on your head, you can start living like you are skipping across the piano and making a beautiful tune with your life. That's right. When you understand how the brain works, how your psychology, biology, neurology, and environment all feed into your brain, and how you can adjust these areas of your life to better serve your brain—you can change your whole life. Sounds simple, right? It kind of is. The hard part is actually doing it.

If you're the type of person with a logical mind who loathes being told to ride out the wave, and paint everything with positivity as you hum and mantra your way to calmness, you and I will get along just swell. This book is focused on tools and strategies that will appeal to us left-brained folk. And if you're into rubbing crystals together by candlelight, we have a drop of that in here for you too...but just a drop.

So let's hop to it, shall we?

If you are ready to start enjoying the good things life has to offer—like, you know, breathing at a normal rate—then it is time for you to get started. Remember, take your time and enjoy the process. You are not just reclaiming your normal respiratory rate, you're reclaiming your life here—which is no easy feat, but it is certainly achievable and worth the effort.

PART 1

WHY DO I FEEL SO SCREWED-UP?

CHAPTER 1

WHY IN THE HECK??

JUST LIKE EVERYONE is a unique and beautiful snowflake (at least that's what my grandma keeps telling me, usually after tough breakups), everyone's anxiety is also unique. It can be caused by a unique cocktail of various reasons or triggers. Anxiety is not a clear-cut, identical experience for every person, which is why there are so many proposed solutions out there when it comes to dealing with this bitch—I mean...issue.

Unfortunately, a ridiculously large number of these solutions revolve around "just thinking positive" and closing your eyes for ten minutes a day while you try in vain not to think about everything that is freaking you out. While meditation and positive thinking can and do work for many people, in many cases, they are not actually explained well enough in the context of a clear reason as to why people are experiencing anxiety in the first place. Instead, many people attempt to prescribe these tools in a way that overlooks the anxiety's root causes entirely and leaves the person suffering feeling as though they have to attempt to simply abandon or repress their anxiety, which...you guessed it...only leads to further anxiety.

In better understanding causes, we can better understand effects. And in better understanding effects, we can better control them. So let's briefly take a look at what I call *The Shitty Four*—that's four general, overarching reasons why we experience anxiety. These four reasons will give you a general explanation as to what is going on inside of you whenever you experience that crippling feeling that's difficult to release and hard to stop from building up in an unhealthy way. You will notice that these reasons go deeper than just having a "noisy brain" or "having a lot on your plate." There are actual concrete, science-backed reasons for why your anxiety exists and what its probable causes are. So yeah, let's get science-y...but just a little bit. I never cared for Science in school. Recess was my personal favorite.

Psychological Reasons For Anxiety

Psychology accounts for the mind, and how the mind works, typically around thoughts and memories. This is less about the physical makeup of the brain and more about how the brain itself actually works in terms of developing consciousness and awareness in the human mind. When it comes to anxiety, psychology is often one of the first things that people look into, as anxiety is often believed to be connected to thoughts and mental processes.

This is where we start to see recurring intrusive thoughts and potential aversions to certain situations or triggers known to cause anxiety in one's life. This can often be caused by past trauma or negative experiences. People usually develop psychological anxiety as a result of the brain perceiving something as dangerous or threatening and then turning the said thing into a trigger, which then stimulates anxiety any time that trigger is perceived. The idea here is to allow your mind to identify the threat and have the necessary energy required to flee or fight off the threat, thus protecting you and keeping you alive. Sounds pretty useful, right? Well, unfortunately, most modern day threats are merely false perceptions and are not actually going to kill you or threaten your survival. But that doesn't stop it from feeling that way.

Biological Reasons For Anxiety

Biological reasons for anxiety are more so relating to actual brain chemistry or the physical state of your body. Often, biological anxiety is caused by hormonal or chemical imbalances which can result in your brain and body not having what they need in order to function in an optimal way. Your brain can then perceive this imbalance as a threat and begin to develop anxiety as a way to give you the energy and awareness required to fulfill whichever need is being overlooked in order to restore balance to the body and eliminate the anxiety.

Unfortunately, most of us are not actually aware of the fact that this is happening, so we may end up overlooking the importance of physically balancing our bodies out to eliminate the existence of anxiety. Furthermore, some people have actual conditions that are either developed or inherited, which may make it challenging for them to develop a healthy balance within their body, thus making biological anxiety difficult for them to heal. In many cases, biological anxiety is treated with lifestyle management and sometimes medications which allow you to bring balance to that temple of yours—your body, that is.

Neurological Reasons For Anxiety

Unlike biological brain function which is based on how your brain operates as a part of your entire system, neurological brain functions are based exclusively on how the brain actually functions. What I mean is this: When we look at neurological functions, it's less about paying attention to how the brain is functioning alongside other organs, but instead about how the brain is responding and functioning as an independent organ.

For example, the transmitters that cause thoughts to flow through your brain or cause your brain to stimulate certain parts of your nervous system are part of neurological processes. Neurological reasons for anxiety often come down to your brain having faulty neural pathways that are not serving your ability to have healthy thoughts and emotional management practices. When you have neurological anxiety, often your brain has literally been wired to experience anxiety, worry, and stress more than what would be normal. This could have occurred in response to a traumatic event or prolonged exposure to stress, which causes your brain to develop these patterns, thus making anxiety your immediate response to various experiences or perceptions.

Lifestyle Reasons For Anxiety

The aforementioned reasons for anxiety all have one thing in common—in a way, they're not your fault. If you're the kind of person who likes a scapegoat, then you're not going to like this section. Because your anxiety could be 100% your fault, and you could have been putting yourself through mental hell all this time for no good reason. How so, you ask?

Well, a major cause for anxiety can actually be your environment and lifestyle, which for many people is a large reason why they develop this unwanted mental condition. You may develop it as a response to a messy environment, an environment that is full of unhealthy triggers, an environment that has you surrounded by unhealthy relationships, or a lifestyle that brings you into these elements regularly. If your physical surroundings, relationships, and circumstances are not healthy, chances are that your environment, and maybe even your lifestyle, are causing you to have negative emotional responses.

CHAPTER 2

TYPES OF ANXIETY

IN ADDITION to there being various *causes* for anxiety, there are also many *types* of anxiety. Having insight into what these causes and types are will give you insight into what symptoms you're having and how those symptoms can be managed or eliminated. In this chapter, we are going to briefly explore what the different types of anxiety are so that you can get a better feel for what type of chaos you are dealing with inside of that overwhelmed brain of yours.

At this point, when you hear something that rings a bell, all you really need to do is make a mental note of what sounds closest to what you are experiencing so that you know what you are going to be working on healing in the future. And identifying what type of crazy you are dealing with will help you get a better grip on what you're going to be up against.

Generalized Anxiety Disorder

Often shortened to "GAD," generalized anxiety disorder results in people feeling bouts of anxiety and overwhelm on a daily basis. People who experience GAD find themselves constantly worrying throughout the day, often to the point that they adopt the tendency to worry as a part of their identity or personality type.

If you are one of the 6.8 million Americans that the Anxiety and Depression Association of America claims has GAD, you may go back and forth between feeling like a total badass superhero who is confident and capable of leaping tall buildings in a single bound, and feeling like a weak pathetic loser who doesn't deserve anything and will never make anything of yourself and will be instantaneously forgotten when you die. Yeah, it can feel dramatic.

You may find yourself worrying about everything from whether or not you said the right thing in that conversation with your friend, to whether anyone's going to show up to your birthday dinner, if your friends are going to drop you when they find out you're not actually cool, whether or not you are worthy enough of the adoration of your crush at work who won't seem to give you the time of day, if said crush saw the broccoli in your teeth from today's super greens salad when you finally worked up the courage to talk to them, whether or not you'll die alone because you chose to eat a super greens salad instead of a cheeseburger and that broccoli in your teeth cost you the love of your life...Yeah, stuff like that.

It doesn't always have to make actual sense. In fact, when

you really look into it, it rarely does. But you still feel it. Oftentimes, the source of the anxiety is fairly minimal or even irrelevant, and if you were asked to logically look at the reason for your anxiety and tell someone why you're feeling what you're feeling and thinking what you're thinking, you'd probably hesitate because it would seem embarrassingly small or unimportant. But still, you can't seem to help yourself and you're just going to continue to worry about it anyway.

Those with GAD tend to behave in a way that expresses nervousness, such as fidgeting obsessively, becoming clumsy during more nervous moments, or doing silly things like walking into a closed door because you were too nervous to pay attention. Ever seen a bird fly into a glass door and knock itself out cold? Yeah, I've been that bird.

A person with GAD may feel or behave accident prone and then may use that to feed their anxiety even further because they are constantly worried about what people think of them and how they are being perceived and judged by others.

Social Anxiety

Social anxiety is a form of anxiety that people experience when they're...well, social...or even more likely, when they're *not* social because they're afraid to be. Perhaps not surprisingly, Larry Cohen, Chair of the National Social Anxiety Center, states that social anxiety usually starts early—as early as age 13, around the age adolescents are transitioning to high school.

But no matter when social anxiety strikes in one's life, it can either happen when you're around other people, or avoiding being around other people. Social anxiety can range in how it shows up, so some people are not even aware of the fact that they have it unless it shows up in a big way.

For example, some people only feel anxious when they are surrounded by a big crowd or by people they do not know, whereas other people feel it even when they are surrounded by the people that they know and love. Some people may even find themselves being okay with being around people one day and then need to be completely isolated the next. In more severe cases, you may have to leave a group situation because you feel like you cannot breathe, or you may feel guilty for dropping out of group plans because someone unexpected chose to show up.

The truth is that social anxiety is extremely common, and chances are, the people you're anxious about being around because of your own social anxiety, are likely also anxious about being around you because of *their* own social anxiety. They just might be hiding it better than you are. Yeahhh, your sweaty palms, eyes constantly darting away, fidgety hands, and obsessively checking your phone and clinging to it like it's a newborn baby's security blanket are a dead giveaway. No one texted you. Stop pretending like you got an important email so you don't have to talk to anyone.

Performance Anxiety

Performance anxiety, one of the most common fears,

shows up in people who are afraid to be put on the spot. Gallup, an esteemed Washington DC analytics company, uncovered in a 2001 poll that 40% of Americans have performance anxiety. And it affects everyone from the praised professional to the everyday layperson. There's an underlying fear of not being able to do something for someone else, or not being able to do it well. This can show up in more severe ways, or in ways that are less severe but still inconvenient or embarrassing to say the least.

For example, you may get performance anxiety only when you are being summoned to speak in front of a crowd or give a professional presentation in front of your superiors. Or, it may strike at random or awkward times such as when you need to do something normal in the year 2020, like I don't know, tie your shoe on a date, or uh... ahem..."seal the deal" if you know what I mean. You can't see it, but I'm raising my eyebrows over here.

Performance anxiety often arises because people feel like they are going to make a fool of themselves in front of others, and it may be worsened if they have evidence that they will based on something having happened in their past. If you once had trouble tying your shoes well on a date, you may now have anxiety every time it's time to tie your shoes...on a date. You can take that literally or metaphorically...if you know what I mean. You can't see it, but I'm raising my eyebrows over here.

The reality is: performance anxiety makes your performance worse, which can make your anxiety worse, which can make your performance even worse, which will probably make your anxiety even worse...and you can see where this spiral ends up. It ain't pretty.

Circumstantial Anxiety

Some people have anxiety caused by something specific, and nothing else. They're usually totally put together, and cool as a cucumber, but when a certain situation comes up, everything goes to shit. This type of anxiety can be caused by having a single, really big, bad experience, or a series of small bad experiences, associated with something in particular.

For example, maybe the last time you tried to do something romantic for your partner, you made a fool of yourself, and now, you are afraid of trying again for fear of being laughed at or made fun of for your blunder. Alternatively, maybe a certain douchebag in your social circle—why you have you a douchebag in your social circle, I don't know, more on that later, but just go with the illustration—but maybe this certain douchebag made fun of you one day, perhaps even jokingly, in front of your friends, and everybody laughed...but you. So now every time that person joins group outings, you feel like you're going to be teased, and it makes you feel down about yourself—so now, that person gives you anxiety.

Or maybe a friend told you your boyfriend or girlfriend was cheating on you, so now, even though that crappy ex of yours is no longer in your life, every time you see that friend, you get uneasy about your current relationship, even though it may be absolutely perfect and be the stuff

Nicholas Sparks movies are made of. Maybe your dad called one time and broke bad news to you about someone in your family, so now every time your phone rings and his name pops up, you get anxiety, anticipating the worst. Or you had a roller-skating accident, so now roller-skates give you the creeps. Ok, that's enough examples, I think you get it. Circumstantial anxiety can be identified by having an aversion to a certain situation or experience that's tied to a similar experience from your past.

CHAPTER 3

WHY YOUR ANXIETY GETS WORSE

AS IF ANXIETY isn't bad enough, sometimes, it can even get worse. This self-help book is really starting to make you feel better, huh? Chances are, you are well aware of the magnitude of the anxious beast. It can exhaust you, tire you out, and burden you with an existence of perpetual high stress, and low energy, leaving you feeling like you're being whipped around by anxiety like a tetherball being slapped around by rambunctious, unsupervised children.

And no matter how bad the anxiety is, it gets worse before it ever gets better. And there are two reasons for that—luckily, two reasons that you are in control of: lack of awareness, and habitual response. Without awareness, how can you solve any problem? And without acknowledging, challenging, and ultimately changing your habitual responses to a problem, how can you make that problem go away? Well, you can't. In the case of anxiety, you'll just be stuck with constant overwhelming feelings and often over-exaggerated responses to triggers that really do not warrant the feeling of a pending heart attack.

Lack Of Awareness

A lack of awareness around what feeds anxiety can cause you to make it even worse without realizing it. Anxiety often walks hand in hand with things like stress and worry, and not realizing this can lead to you accidentally feeding into your issue if your primary focus is just on eliminating anxious feelings and not also eliminating stress and worry. It's like using cold medicine which, sure temporarily can alleviate your symptoms, but it's much more valuable to examine the root and eliminate the cause altogether so the problem doesn't keep coming back. If you manage to ward off the symptoms of problematic anxiety, but you're still doing the same stressful things that cause you to worry to the point of anxiety in the first place, chances are you are going to find yourself right back to where you started—an anxious mess.

Many people go through their lives unconsciously, never taking the time to pause or self-reflect. So they don't realize what exactly is stressing them out, or what things they typically have stressful responses to, which can lead to them constantly feeding their problems, completely ignorant to what they're actually doing or the mental and emotional consequences of it. Basically, they become that innocent, unwitting child eating an ice cream cone and then having their dog scoop up big bites every time they look away. When they turn back, they see their ice cream is gone, they're upset about it, they want the ice cream back, but they still don't know why it's gone, so they continue to unknowingly remain prey to the very thing that's taking away the thing they want most.

As an adult, the ice cream is your mental health, and the dog is every little trigger for stress and worry. Later in this book, we'll discuss some things you can do to identify these triggers so you're not that person sitting in the corner stabbing themselves with a pencil and then crying every time they realize it hurts. We'll see how you can stop sitting in the corner feeding your anxiety with stress and worry and then crying every time it ends in a full-blown panic attack, or a little field trip to the hospital where the nurses all side-eye you for letting yourself get so far gone.

Habitual Response

Another reason why your anxiety can be so bad and unrelenting is your habitual response. If you have a long history of having anxious responses to circumstances, triggers, adulting, or just plain life, you have pretty much perfected the practice of working yourself up into a respectable panic attack.

Think about a child or a baby. At one point, it knew nothing about anxiety. All of its needs were taken care of. Everyone cared how it felt and bent over backwards to keep it happy. People responded to its every beck and call and it got everything it could possibly ever want just by... crying. (Don't you miss those times?) Then this one time, it felt threatened in some way, and it had an anxious emotional response to that apparent threat, and somehow, it felt like that response actually served its needs in one way or another.

After a while, it realized that it was really good at this behavior, and the repeated performance of that particular behavior in response to that particular threat became more and more ingrained, turning into a habit that now happens without any thought or consideration. Now, any time that trigger pops up, it instinctually responds, not even giving logic a chance to intervene. And this carries over into adulthood and turns the baby into a mess of a grownup human. And this is all done at the expense of mental health.

In order for you to break a habit, you need to teach your old dog a new trick—that new trick being to stop bugging out every time a totally casual experience is for no good reason perceived as a life-threatening event that will either end in you dying or the end of the world...or both. You can do that by following the upcoming tactics in this very book, and getting your brain newly accustomed to having healthy, functional, and productive responses to what used to be anxiety-inducing triggers.

CHAPTER 4

FEELING BAD ABOUT FEELING BAD

DESPITE HOW COMMON ANXIETY IS, there are hordes of people living in the closet so to speak, because they are too afraid to admit that they suffer from anxiety. And this added layer of feeling bad about feeling bad can make things feel even worse than they actually are. Plus, the denial that can occur as a result, can stop people from seeking or getting the help they need to make positive change.

For some reason, a great deal of shame seems to go along with people admitting that sometimes certain things are not as easy for them to engage in as they might be for other people. But, the thing is, that's the case for literally everyone. Everyone has at least one thing that makes their pulse increase more than it does for the next guy. And conversely, everyone has at least one thing where they can totally keep their cool, while the next guy's heart is racing uncontrollably. But still, for whatever reason, people value stoicism and emotional impermeability over acknowledging hardships and attempting to work with yourself to experience a greater sense of calm and wellbeing in your life. The irony there is that the latter takes more courage than the former.

In our society, there is a huge misconception that we are always supposed to be strong all the time and that experiencing any level of weakness is a sign that there is something seriously wrong with us and that we need to get serious help. In many cases, although anxiety is having serious adverse consequences in our lives, it doesn't even always require quote-on-quote "serious help"—it just requires self-management and self-monitoring so that you can work through your symptoms and find your own peace and solace. But none of that process can take place if you continue living in denial because of your shame.

There is nothing shameful about admitting that you have a hard time and that sometimes you need to approach life or certain situations in a different way than the average person because it brings out a more challenging response in you. If someone has an issue with you for owning your problems, that is a reflection of them, not a reflection of you. Realize that anyone who responds poorly to your anxiety is likely just having a hard time with compassion, or even more likely, they have shame around their own emotions and anxiety, and they feel uncomfortable with the fact that you do not. There is no reason to fear that people will treat you differently if you open up about your struggles. On the other hand, they'll likely feel relieved and open up to you about their own, or offer you suggestions and help with yours. And anyone who doesn't, you know that is a person you need to simply cut out of your life.

When we are unwilling to own our mental health challenges, we find ourselves denying that they exist, which can lead to even further challenges in the future. The more you deny it, the more you find yourself growing even more anxious. Your anxiety becomes even more powerful as it attempts to run its course, yet is being denied. And you are cultivating new anxiety around the idea of anxiety itself. Through this, your anxiety becomes its very own trigger, which you can imagine how that's definitely not helping things. Owning your anxiety allows you to admit to yourself and those around you that you need help, or that you need to do certain things differently so that you can engage in life in a way that does not have you trapped by anxiety's whim. When you own it, you actually give yourself the permission that you need to work with yourself and your emotional experiences so that you can create peace and freedom in your life.

Release Your Shame

Women are supposed to save face when they are struggling, and men are supposed to be strong enough that they never even struggle in the first place. Sound familiar? Probably so. Sound ridiculous? It should. Somehow, as a society, we have found a way to make it seem like literally everyone is required to behave in a certain, unbothered, unemotional manner unless we want to find themselves being subjected to bullies or the harsh judgment of others.

See, out in society, there are people who downplay the severity of anxiety. These are people who haven't experienced it themselves (or who have but are either in denial or not in tune enough with themselves to realize they suffer too). But this school of people tend to think that someone can simply "be positive" or "think positive thoughts" or what have you, and suddenly be magically cured. "Like, yeah, thanks, I never thought of that, I'll just think a happy thought, let me get on that right now. Oh look, I'm magically cured!" Yeah, no.

Overcoming anxiety does not happen like that. It takes time and consistency to make it go away just like it took time and consistency to get it there in the first place. Anxiety is a series of triggers that have been wired into your brain through neurological pathways and repeated psychological behaviors. You quite literally need to rewire your brain if you are going to find lasting freedom from your sometimes crippling symptoms. So don't allow ignorant people's dismissal of the reality of what you're going through make you feel shameful or embarrassed.

To release your shame around having anxiety, own the fact that it is real. Don't let people convince you that you're "making it all up." Know that it's real and be willing to trust in yourself and believe in your ability to both recognize and overcome it, even if the people around you are not quite as compassionate. At the end of the day, you are going to run into people who are extremely ignorant about what it is that you are dealing with and who will be unwilling to find any way to have compassion for you and what you are going through.

The more you focus on these people, the worse you are going to feel about yourself and your struggles. If, however, you turn your eyes away from people who don't get it, and focus on the ones who do, you will likely find that you are surrounded by far more compassionate and understanding people than you expected. Then, the more you experience these compassionate interactions and relationships, the better you are going to feel about yourself and what you are going through, as you come to realize that it is absolutely nothing to be ashamed of.

Learn To Talk About It With Others

Communicating with others about how you are feeling and what you are going through not only gives them the opportunity to be compassionate towards you, but it also allows them to be sensitive to your triggers and better accommodate what you are feeling. If you don't want your social butterfly coworker to keep forcing you to go to huge parties and networking events, you are going to have to talk to her about your anxiety.

While opening up can seem to be easier with a close friend or family member, sometimes, it can actually be more difficult because of the layered challenges involved. If you have social anxiety or any other anxiety around talking with people or having difficult conversations, talking about that anxiety can prove to be extra challenging. Fortunately, there are many ways that you can clue people in so they have an idea as to what is going on.

One of the best ways to start is to talk to people who already know you fairly well, as these are people who likely already know that you have anxiety anyway, even though you haven't admitted it to them yet. Focus on talking to the ones who are most likely to respond in a positive and compassionate manner. If they truly care about you, the conversation will go well, and you'll build up the confidence to open up to others as needed once you know that you've had a positive experience where you were well-received.

You can also find a compassionate close friend or family to be your confidant so that when you do decide to tell other people, you now have someone to confide in about your fears or hesitations around it. This not only gives you a chance to let them be your cheerleader and encourage you, but also, if someone else does meet you with ignorance or a lack of compassion, you can turn to your confidant and talk it out. This is an good opportunity for you to start overcoming your fears and creating a greater sense of support and authenticity in your social circle while growing your closest relationships even closer.

Make It Not Such A Big Deal

Finally, part of owning your anxiety is learning how to make it not such a big deal. When you talk about something like it is some big huge *National Enquirer* cover scandal, people are obviously going to react in a big way and make a huge deal out of it. As someone with anxiety, having people respond in this grandiose way can feel uncomfortable and can make it harder for you to open up to anyone. You may find yourself feeling anxious about what they think about you or how they feel about you now that you have told them, all because you told them with some big elaborate attitude rather than keeping it calm and relaxed. Telling people that you have anxiety does not need to be done in the same way that you would tell someone that their loved one has cancer or their dog got run over. It also does not need to be scandalous like their best friend cheated on their boyfriend or their boss was having a high-class affair with an escort. Fueling energy of drama and scandal into your admission of anxiety is only going to add more drama and scandal, which could lead to people responding in a way that may make you feel uncomfortable.

Learning how to make things more casual comes from owning it yourself first, and realizing that it is a part of you, but is not the complete definition of who you are. And telling someone about your anxious feelings doesn't make you any different than you were before—you are just more willing to admit what you are going through to both yourself and others now. This does not change how you behave or what you think or feel—it simply means that you may be more open with people now so that when they are doing something that crosses your boundary you can feel more comfortable to speak up and prevent it. And better yet, they'll be more conscious of your boundaries and not put you in situations where they can be tested. Or, maybe if you are going to skip out on something due to anxiety, you can actually admit that it is because of your anxiety and not because your Grandmother's cat died and you have to attend its funeral...in Tanzania. So when it comes to opening up about what you're going through, be honest and keep it casual. You'll be glad you did.

PART 2

GETTING ACQUAINTED WITH THE PROBLEM

CHAPTER 5

STRESS

WE KNOW that stress can contribute to your anxiety. I'm sure you see this on a daily or perhaps hourly basis in your own life. For many people, stress is the first stage right before an anxious spiral breaks out. Stress does not only contribute to anxiety in an obvious way by creating an overwhelming number of thoughts and experiences in your mind, but stress creates anxiety by having your entire body and chemistry actually physically change in order to accommodate for the emotion of stress and the impact that it is meant to have on your body.

Why We Have Emotions

I hate emotions. Especially during sappy movies with my mom. But contrary to what some of the fellow emotion haters like me may think, emotions do actually have a purpose. See, emotions are actually chemical responses within the body that help you generate the right amount of energy, feelings, and thoughts in order to respond appropriately to a situation. When they are functioning optimally, your emotions will help you discover what you should and should not be doing based on what makes you feel negative, neutral, or positive. Surely, you could see how this could be useful.

For example, if you do something and it makes you feel sad, you know that you do not want to do it again because sadness sucks. It causes pain. And pain hurts. Alternatively, if you do something and it makes you feel excited, you know that you may want to do that again because excitement is fun and it feels like an emotional high.

Stress is an emotion that is intended to show you that you are doing something that could potentially be harmful or overwhelming for your body. Some types of stress lead us to feel as though we are in a dangerous situation that could be life-threatening, and other types of stress can indicate that we are taking on too much and we are not honoring the needs of our mind or body.

For example, if you're hiking in the woods, and you come across a mountain lion roaring and baring its teeth, that could be dangerous. That could be stressful. But also, if you take on too many tasks at work, you may begin to feel stressed out because your mind is overwhelmed by the number of things that you need to get done and it may be feeling as though you do not have enough time or energy to complete those tasks. Because you know that there is likely going to be a negative consequence to you not completing your tasks, stress begins to develop because you do not want to face the consequence of not being able to complete everything that you need to get done. When you think your job is on the line, you're going to get fired, go bankrupt, and live under a bridge, that could be just as stressful as that mountain lion.

How Stress Affects Your Body

Now that you understand the meaning of emotions and what stress indicates, let's start learning about what it does to your body. Stress affects your body by triggering the production of the hormones cortisol and adrenaline. Cortisol is specifically linked to stress itself, whereas adrenaline is produced any time we experience an emotion that results in us requiring or having heightened energy levels. As these two hormones are produced, your body begins to have specific reactions in response to them, which are intended to help you use that stress to save your life, essentially.

Well, if you were a gazelle in the savannah being hunted by a lion, they would save your life, as they would give you the energy that you need to high tail it out of there before the big kitty eats you. These days, as modern day humans, the only time stress really serves us from an actual survival perspective, is with that sudden massive wave of adrenaline that it surges through our system when we are about to get hit by a car or when something nearly takes us out of the game, so that we can jump out of the way and live to tell the tale. Otherwise, the body's physical manifestation of stress doesn't really do as much good as it used to.

Once stress does heighten in the body, you begin to experience symptoms like a quickened pulse, heart palpitations, tense muscles, heightened awareness, and a surge of energy. You might begin to feel chest pain or even fatigue if you are extremely stressed, as that much energy pulsing through your body can be exhausting. To your body, it feels like you just lived an entire day in a single second.

As stress continues to pulse through your body, you may feel a need to leap into action and do something, which for some people can trigger them to either get moving on what actually needs to be done, or start filling their life up with "so-called" stress relieving crutches which end up producing more stress in the long run. This is when you find people who smoke like a chimney, spend hours a day at the gym doing burpees and deadlifts, or expend energy engaging in any other nervous habit to pass the time and work off their stress, when what they need to do is just complete their unfinished tasks, thereby getting rid of what's causing the stress in the first place. Those three hours spent doing burpees could have been three hours spent knocking out that presentation that's looming in the back of your mind. No one can actually do burpees for three hours, but you get the point.

Excessive and prolonged exposure to stress can lead to a myriad of things, as constantly high levels of cortisol in your body can lead to increased risk of heart disease and things like dementia or Alzheimer's in the long run. In the short term, it can cause things like digestive issues, headaches, anxiety, altered sex drive, overwhelm, anger, sadness, depression, social withdrawal, restlessness, and sleep problems. None of these are pleasant to deal with, so getting your stress in control and releasing your stress-related anxiety in a way that makes sense is necessary if you want to prevent yourself from having serious issues in the future, whether short term, or long term.

Why It Can Be Hard To Neutralize Stress

You might be wondering, if stress can literally drop you into your grave, why are people not working harder to eliminate the stress from their lives? The answer to this is simple: most people think they are, or they have blind spots to their problem areas and triggers. Even though most people feel like they have their backs against the wall in various situations, they simply do not see what particular things or people are actively feeding into their stress levels, so they continue behaving as if there is nothing wrong. The reality is that there is something wrong—and the longer they ignore it or fail to identify it, the worse their stress and anxiety are going to get.

In order to neutralize stress, you need to know where it is coming from so you don't end up allowing it to continue to grow in the background as you attempt to fix it with Band-aid solutions that never actually make a big difference in the long run. The true path to eliminating stress-induced anxiety is to eliminate the stress. It's like a hair, if you shave a hair, it will come back, because the root of the hair, the follicle, the thing that causes the hair to grow in the first place, is still there just beneath the surface, mocking you, cackling at your naivete, thinking you solved the problem. Immediately after you shave, the hair appears to be gone, but since the follicle is still in tact right below the surface, it's coming right on back.

In the case of stress, attacking the "follicle" will entail making lifestyle changes that mean adjusting your environment, your relationships, your obligations, your physical responses to life, your emotional responses, and your mental responses. As you adjust these areas of your life, you will find that it becomes easier for you to have more meaningful responses to life in general. Rather than always keeping low amounts of stress running in the background of your life and simply trying to suppress it or hide from it, you can acknowledge the stress, release it, and then live a generally stress-free life.

Understand that the goal is not to eliminate the stress response altogether, but to eliminate residual stress and the prolonged negative feelings or consequences that happen as a result of the biological stress response. We're here to create a more "low-impact" lifestyle that will not amplify your stress overall. The more you allow yourself to have a generally stress-free lifestyle, the less intense your response to stress will be when it comes up and rears its ugly head.

As a result, you'll begin to have a more positive life in general, and your anxiety will begin to fade away as you no longer feel as though you constantly need to be on high alert all the time to handle what's on your plate. From this state, any time stress is triggered, you can recognize it, respond to the root of the trigger from a place of logic and calm, and then allow yourself to move forward and continue on with your otherwise peaceful lifestyle.

Something To Think About

As mentioned in the intro, at the end of each chapter in this section of the book, we will end with a few reflection questions to help you get more familiar with what's really going on with you. This is a good place to make sure you have a pen, paper, stylus, tablet, keyboard, laptop, feather, scroll—whatever you're into for note taking.

Throughout this book, we provide some other anxiety solutions that also involve writing things down, so whatever you choose to use for these reflection questions, you can also use for implementing some of those upcoming strategies later on. You can get one notebook or journal singularly used for this purpose, and think of it as your own personal little *get your shit together* journal. Pause any time you need to take a moment to write something down. Don't feel rushed. This book will always be here when you get back.

And now, here are the reflection questions for this section:

1. What's something you've been putting off that you know you need to do, but has been put on the mental backburner and keeps finding its way at the bottom of your ever-growing to-do list?
2. Are there any people in your life that cause you undue stress?
3. Realizing that stress is simply what we feel in

reaction to a fear of an undesired outcome, what are your biggest fears that cause stress?

4. What do you usually do when you feel stressed? And is it healthy physically, mentally, or emotionally?

CHAPTER 6

HABITS AND BEHAVIOR

OUR HABITS and behaviors can have a major impact on the anxiety that we experience in our lives. As a matter of fact, our habits and behaviors and our stress often correlate with each other, as many times, we have habits or behaviors that we are engaging in that are impacting our long-term stress levels. Many people believe that stress comes from the mind, but it can also come from the body when we find ourselves treating our bodies like they are replaceable.

If your friends call you Guzzling Gary because you down a six-pack and a dozen shots every other night, you are exposing your body to stress and creating an increase in your natural stress response. Shocking, right? You cannot binge drink for weeks on end and then expect yourself to feel a hundred percent afterward. What do Calculus, waking up at 5 am, and crushing it in a job interview have in common? These are all things that do not happen after a night of binge drinking.

You cannot escape the natural consequences of your actions. Most people live in complete lack of awareness of their actions, and in complete denial of the consequences of those actions. They are unknowingly and consistently engaging in behaviors that cause physical and mental stress, thereby exacerbating anxiety.

Drinking habits are not the only habits that might be stressing you out, either. Sometimes, our problem lies in doing something, and other times, our problem lies in *not* doing something. I'm talking procrastination and laziness. Any habit that prevents you from moving forward or achieving your goals in life can greatly contribute to your anxiety in many different ways.

First of all, having something in the back of your mind and having things undone is a constant stressor. We don't realize how unfinished tasks can cause mental strain. It's a mental burden knowing there are things you are supposed to be doing, but you are not doing them. Also, as humans, we all have standards for what we want to do, have, and be. We have in mind a certain level of what we want to be like as people and what we want our lives to look like. When we don't live up to those standards and our lives are not in alignment with our vision, we can actually produce stress within ourselves because we are behaving in a way that prevents us from achieving our personal standards.

At the root of this, especially when trying to do something that can somehow elevate your life, can lie a subconscious belief that we are unable to or unworthy of achieving those standards. So we behave in a way that sabotages our ability to achieve our vision for ourselves and our lives, which can turn into a spiral of self-loathing and disappointment, thus creating even more anxiety within us.

We all have self-sabotaging behaviors. And sometimes we use these self-sabotaging behaviors as coping mechanisms to deal with our anxiety. Maybe you like to smoke after a tough day at work, drink "casually" to calm you down so you feel comfortable talking to people, or watch an entire season of a show on Netflix when you feel alone. These behaviors can seem harmless, but I hate to break it to you... they're not.

Not only are they harmful behaviors when standing alone —we all know smoking isn't exactly a treat for the lungs, drinking alcohol is literally drinking poison that alters the state of your mind and reduces cognitive ability and the ability to make good decisions, and watching TV endlessly is a great way to kill brain cells—but it's all harmful on a psychological level as well. You're basically training your brain to take an uncomfortable situation, and instead of facing it head on and dealing with your shit, you teach your brain to try to numb your feeling of discomfort with an unhealthy habitual action that eventually becomes second nature...which is why you're probably getting mad at me right now.

At this point, you may find yourself really digging in your heels: *But I always feel better after I do it, so why on Earth would I stop? And if I feel better afterwards, how could it be bad for my anxiety? There has got to be another way for me to get around this so that I can keep engaging in this habit or behavior.*

If you are having these thoughts, you need to kick yourself right now, because you are holding yourself back. Attempting to justify and hold on to the behaviors that in the long run do you more harm than good and indirectly cause stress is just like you attempting to justify and hold on to your anxiety, which sounds absolutely ridiculous... because it is ridiculous. If you are fine living stressed, anxious, and keeping everything just as it is, then, by all means, continue engaging in these self-sabotaging behaviors that have you living beneath your personal standards.

But, if you want to start feeling like you actually have some control over yourself and your life, then you need to look at your habits closely, loosen up on the ones that don't serve you, and start giving yourself the opportunity to learn and grow. For some of your habits, it'll be sufficient to pull back (hint: watching TV), but for other habits, you just need to stop altogether (hint: smoking). Remember what we said: you cannot escape consequence. Your objective when it comes to overcoming anxiety relating to your habits and behaviors will be learning how to create improved coping habits for yourself so that you are no longer clinging on to self-sabotaging behaviors to get yourself through moments of anxiety.

Now, this process may be easier said than done. In addition to the fact that your mind is attached to these patterns and behaviors, you also need to understand that your entire life has likely been built around these coping strategies. In many cases, people will make a whole full-blown lifestyle out of it by creating friendships, habits, routines, and hobbies that surround their coping strategies and self-sabotaging behaviors. For example, someone who drinks to cope with their anxiety may befriend people who party on a regular basis so that they have people who are willing to drink with them.

Then, they will spend all of their nights and weekends drinking and partying, partying and drinking, which leads to a sense of fulfillment in terms of having their anxiety released and their social needs fulfilled in the short term. But really, they're setting themselves up for steep disappointment in themselves for not living according to their true standards, and in the process, making their emotional problems deeper in the long term.

Attempting to shift your habits when your entire lifestyle is built around them can be challenging. There may be people, places, and things you have to get rid of, and there are often some uncomfortable conversations to be had. But it's all worth it. Don't be afraid to put yourself first and decide the best way that you can effectively put new strategies in place to help you make your shifts towards a more peaceful life.

It is also important that you understand that your self-sabotaging behaviors are not always obvious or straightforward, even if it seems like they should be, so they may be difficult to identify at first. But it's okay and perfectly natural for this process to take time. These destructive patterns have kept you feeling safe for as long as you have been doing them, so teaching yourself that there is an alternative safe route won't happen overnight. But trust yourself. Your mind may be afraid, thinking that you are about to chuck yourself off a metaphorical cliff, but just tell it you actually have better plans in place. As you continue creating this new awareness and instilling new habits into your mind, you will find that it becomes a lot easier for you to trust in yourself and the new coping methods that you choose to teach yourself. As a result, you will be able to change your patterns and engage in healthier strategies that support you long term.

Something To Think About

1. What was an action you did in the last week that had a consequence you didn't like?
2. Are you living up to your standards for yourself? If not, how not and why not?
3. What people, places, and things do you ultimately need to get rid of to ensure that you are living up to your personal standards?
4. What's a bad habit you've been wanting to break?
5. Do you have any self-sabotaging habits or behaviors?
6. In what ways does your lifestyle support your worst habits?

CHAPTER 7

PERSONALITY

THIS CAN BE one of the hardest pills to swallow, but sometimes, people who have anxiety experience it because of their personality type. That's right. Sometimes, you have anxiety because you are just an anxious little basket case, and that's all there is to it. Just kidding. Personality type can be natural and innate to some degree, but there are also some personality *traits* or certain actions that can highlight or exacerbate a personality type. The good news is, personality traits can be learned, so they can also be unlearned. And actions can be consciously done, so they can also be consciously undone.

Some people, for instance, such as people pleasers and natural worrying types, find themselves experiencing increased anxiety because they are prone to trying to do too much, or stress themselves out trying to please those around them and make sure everyone else is okay. If this is the case for you, you can rest assured that even though anxiety is a natural side effect of who you are, there are still solutions that you can implement to cope and stop feeling overwhelmed.

If you find that you have a personality type that contributes to anxiety by making you naturally more nervous than other people, you may benefit from spending time getting to know what parts of your personality are contributing to your anxious feelings. Since personality is learned, oftentimes you will find that the parts of your personality that are contributing to your anxiety were learned, too, meaning that you can actually thank your weird parents or that crazy baby-sitter you had when you were six for your strange, anxious behaviors. The more you engaged in these behaviors over time, the deeper they became rooted in who you were, which lead to you identifying with these behaviors. As a result, you find yourself regularly engaging in them and maybe even believing that you cannot rid yourself of them, but that's not the case.

The important thing to understand is that, although it can be more challenging, your personality can actually shift and grow over time. This means that you do not have to be an anxious little ball of crazy for your entire life, but instead, you can actually take control over yourself and shift your personality into one that serves you in enjoying life more. The best way to do this is to begin focusing on neurological and psychological strategies for healing from anxiety so that you can actually rewire your brain and chill out. (More on that later in Parts 4 and 5.)

If you think about it that way, personalities are changeable and malleable. Think about it—you have likely known someone at some point in your life who met someone else and instantly began behaving as if they were an entirely new person. The changes may have been positive or negative in your eyes, but judgments aside, you were able to witness noticeable changes in this person. Maybe your best friend started dating someone new and seemingly changed overnight, or your loved one or acquaintance experienced some significant event in their life that caused them to shift.

Sometimes, these shifts are only temporary and the individual switches back to their "original self" after a short period of time, and other times these shifts can be long-lasting and even permanent. Often, the shifts will remain permanent if they are being triggered to be reinforced in the psyche over and over again, as this is actually how personality traits are developed in the first place. So, if you were consistently told that you were unworthy as a child, you would have had this trigger reinforced so many times that as an adult you feel yourself behaving and feeling in alignment with a person who is unworthy, thereby shaping your personality and identity, and present and future actions.

So it's likely that many of your anxiety-inducing personality traits, ranging from things like being unreasonably shy to being a people pleaser or a worrywart, all stem back to some event or relationship from when you were younger. Making adjustments to shift the parts of your personality that make you anxious takes time and practice, just as it took time and practice for you to get this way in the first place.

But rest assured, you can do it. Stay tuned for Parts 3, 4, and 5, which are dedicated to actionable practices and strategies. There, you will learn about what you can do to start adjusting your psyche to eliminate anxiety, nervousness, and stress from your personality style. And in the meantime, get ready for the reflection questions at the end of this chapter to start uncovering ways that you can make changes. Soon enough, you can start feeling like the confident, cool as a cucumber badass that you and I both know you are meant to be!

Something To Think About

1. What personality traits do you have that make your anxiety worse?
2. Of those personality traits, at what point in your life, and from whom did you learn them?
3. What was the most recent person or event that you experienced in your life that impacted your personality for the better?
4. Which part(s) of your personality would you like to shift to ease you anxiety, and who in your life can you model the desired shift after?

CHAPTER 8

POOR SOCIAL SKILLS

SOME PEOPLE ARE NATURALLY GIFTED at being the person everyone wants to come to their party. And some people are naturally gifted (or, cursed) at being the person everyone wants to cancel their party plans over if they find out they're coming. When it comes to social skills, some people have it, and some people don't. And for the people that don't, life can get a little stressful.

Humans crave social connection, which is why it can be kind of strange to consider that most of us are extremely sucky when it comes to engaging effectively in social situations. While some people can get by with their charming good looks, their natural charisma and confidence, and their gift of gab, not everyone can be so lucky as to have these skills at their disposal. In fact, quite a bit of the population has a hard time engaging in positive social interactions with other people. Not only do people simply lack the confidence to charm the pants off everyone they come across, they also lack communication skills essential for speaking up for themselves, getting their point across, having difficult conversations with poise, and disagreeing effectively with others.

Poor social skills do not only lead to empty social calendars and challenging relationships, but they can also lead to straight up anxiety. Many people find themselves anxious to engage in social interactions because they are not confident in how they can effectively communicate with people in a positive or engaging manner. Their ineffective communication has likely also lead to uncomfortable feelings of rejection, unwanted confrontations, or feeling misunderstood by the people around them, all of which can make things even more difficult.

But the thing is, our need to be social truly is a need and not just a want. In fact, our lives kind of depend on it. The Australian Longitudinal Study of Aging found in 2005 that people with the most friends had a tendency to outlive those with the fewest friends by 22%. So getting this whole social thing down can literally be life and death. Okay, I'm sorry, did I scare you? Let's just leave it at this: social connection is important to our longevity and quality of life. But if you have poor social skills, it can make anxiety even worse because you find yourself craving connection while also being too afraid to actually try to make that connection with anyone for fear of rejection or confrontation. This leads to a terrible see-saw of going back and forth between trying to get your social needs fulfilled and trying not to feel like you are that kid that never gets picked for dodgeball.

Naturally, this inner struggle can worsen your anxiety and make your poor social skills an even bigger setback for you. Now, not only are you struggling with having a basic conversation with people, but you are also so nervous that you are coming across even weirder, which leads to even more struggles. This basically never ends until either someone manages to get past your weird eye twitch, dart-y eyes, and weird mumble, and sticks it through with you long enough to learn who you really are and realize you're not actually a creep, or you learn how to ditch your anxious behaviors so that you can avoid coming off as a creep in the first place. The latter is often easier and quicker than the former.

To put it simply, if you want to stop having anxiety relating to your poor social skills, you have to stop being so frickin' awkward and get yourself together. Engaging in healthy self-validation will increase your self-confidence, which will lead to participating in conversations, interactions, and situations with more social confidence. As a result, instead of dreading making eye contact with people and searching the internet for online excuse generators to help you get out of any plans that involve you leaving your house, you'll find yourself actually having fun around people and getting your social needs fulfilled without coming across as ridiculous or weird. (And if you didn't previously know that are websites that will generate random excuses for you to get out of things, and you're now searching for and bookmarking one of those websites in your web browser, that was *not* the point of this section.)

Fortunately, the world of overcoming social anxiety is very forgiving because so many people—according to the ADAA, 15 million in America alone to be exact—live with social anxiety. But let's be honest, despite that statistic, pretty much everyone has felt some form of fear when they are around new people, or experienced some kind of social anxiety to a degree.

Because it's so common, it's actually really easy to find other people who can relate to you and who will be patient with you as you overcome your seemingly incurable awkwardness. As you grow used to owning how challenging this is for you, and practicing ways to overcome it, you will find yourself in more and more situations where you are accepted and well-received, and the more you have these situations of positive social reinforcement, the easier it will become for you to continue having positive social interactions, growing your social skills and confidence even more. That way, if your crush looks at you, you won't wet yourself or collapse into a heart attack....again.

Something To Think About

1. How would you rate your social confidence on a scale of 1 to 10?
2. Do you feel 100% comfortable in social situations with people you don't know?
3. Do you feel 100% comfortable in social situations with people you do know?
4. Do you avoid social invitations? Why, how frequently, and in what way?

5. What behaviors do you engage in when you are in uncomfortable social situations?

6. What exactly is it that you are afraid of in social interactions? What do you fear that other people will perceive you as? What do you fear that people will judge you for?

CHAPTER 9

LOW-QUALITY RELATIONSHIPS

GRANDMA TRIED TO WARN YOU. *That girl's a bad influence. He's a loser. Don't date him, I don't trust him. She'll use you up and bring you down.*

If you've lived long enough, you've been in a low quality relationship. You may have even been the person who was the reason it was a low quality relationship, but that's none of my business. The point is, low-quality relationships are known for causing anxiety, and strangely enough, for many of the same reasons that poor social skills can lead to anxiety. When you are in a relationship with someone, you tend to have a high amount of trust in that person, making things even more dangerous, because the feeling of connection or obligation will cause you to take on more stress from those relationships. Relationships that are considered low-quality and that contribute to anxiety can come in many shapes and sizes, although they will often be centered around similar issues: poor communication and unhealthy emotional connections.

When you are in a relationship without effective communication, or where your emotional needs are not being met, it can be challenging to feel "normal." Many people stay in these relationships because they feel they are not worthy of anything better, or because they dupe themselves into believing that the situation or person will change or improve. In the long run, when we stay in low-quality relationships in order to fulfill an emotional need (often to receive love or validation of our worthiness), we find ourselves adapting in unhealthy ways to attempt to maintain the relationship. Typically, a person staying in a relationship like this worries that they will not be good enough to find what they are looking for elsewhere, so they think they have to contort to fit the relationship and just deal with it.

Many different situations can arise when you feel like you need to settle in low-quality relationships to feel loved and validated. On one end of the scale, you can find yourself repressing parts of who you are in an effort to be validated and well-received by your partner. You may deny your likes, desires, and even your needs in favor of theirs so they will keep you around and continue to make you feel "loved," even though the "love" is often very small and conditional.

This could happen in a platonic, professional, or romantic relationship, but for the sake of this example, let's just say it's happening in a romantic relationship. You may find yourself going out of your way to start liking, doing, or becoming things that are not fulfilling to you because you desire to show the other person that you are loveable. As a result, your entire personality can shift to serve your partner, which can cause you to feel disconnected from who you are.

Since this person you have become to serve your partner is foreign to you, you can begin to feel overwhelmed and anxious because you do not fully understand who it is that you need to be, and you're constantly fighting the switch between who you really are and who you want others to perceive you to be. And it's hard work, switching between multiple identities and trying to manage when to turn each one on or off. And when you get what feels like positive reinforcement from your partner for certain behaviors, the stakes become even higher as you desperately want to protect that feeling of being loved. But you may find yourself experiencing more stress-related anxiety as the parts of yourself that you like are being denied to serve this other person. In many cases, this constant fight to suppress true identity in defense of inauthenticity can lead to mental, emotional, and physical stress, which can further increase your anxiety.

So on one hand, the problem may lie in you trying to be someone you are not for your partner or the other person in the relationship. On the other hand, the problem may lie in you not being the person that your partner wants you to be, and having negative repercussions as a result. Both scenarios sound similar, but there's a slight nuance. For example, if you are in a low-quality relationship with a narcissist or someone who is emotionally unavailable or emotionally abusive, you may find yourself feeling anxious for fear of what will come of having or expressing your own needs or desires. Sometimes, in these relationships, you might find yourself getting ignored or punished for having needs or desires, which can lead to you having anxiety about expressing yourself. The longer you stay in a relationship like this, the greater your anxiety will become and the harder it will be for you to express yourself to other people, even those who are not your abusive or emotionally unavailable partner.

When it comes to low-quality relationships, figuring out how to proceed needs to be done with a very intentional approach. You need to evaluate your situation first, and then choose the best course of action based on your evaluation. If you are in a relationship where you are neglected, or emotionally or physically abused, leaving that relationship quickly and safely will be necessary as the relationship will never change. If you are in a relationship where you are behaving or reacting negatively in a way that is not reflective of the way you are being treated, a different course of action is in order.

For instance, if you act as though your partner is unavailable or unfair to you, but you are behaving this way because of a past relationship, and not your current partner's actions, you need to look at yourself first and try to make adjustments in yourself instead of abandoning the relationship. So when a relationship doesn't feel right, first identify the source. Sometimes, your partner is not the problem, but the behavior that you learned elsewhere is. If you are in a relationship where the main problem is poor communication skills, you can always work together with a willing partner to find out how you can communicate more effectively so that you both find a way to meet on the same page.

The key here is being able to evaluate the difference between low-quality relationships that will never change, and low-quality relationships that can change but so far neither partner has had the awareness or skills to change it. If you are in a relationship where no change can happen, it is important that you recognize this and leave the relationship in order to make your adjustments so that you can begin healing. If you are in a relationship where change can happen, make sure both parties in the relationship are willing to change, and willing to take the necessary steps to start enacting that change, so that you both can begin experiencing more positive outcomes from your relationship. But if you continue to stay in an unhealthy relationship that either cannot change or will not change, you are going to continue experiencing anxiety.

Part of mitigating the anxiety caused from low-quality relationships is doing the work on yourself to validate yourself and see yourself as worthy. You also want to start setting more clear boundaries around what you are and are not willing to accept from people around you, and what you are and are not willing to do, and then enforcing those boundaries. It can be challenging, especially with people who are used to treating you a certain way, but as you continue to draw the line and protect it, you will find that those who truly care about you will adapt. Those who do not will naturally fade away, making room for people who are willing to respect and honor your boundaries and treat you with respect.

If you have never had strong boundaries, enacting this alone can give you a massive boost toward relieving your anxiety. Boundaries are basically like a battle shield, protecting you from the shit that everyone is trying to throw your way. If you are not skilled with your shield, that shit is going to come right through your defensive line and keep hitting you again and again. And who wants to be constantly hit with flying shit? If you do learn how to use that battle shield effectively, however, you can Sparta your way through the battlefield and make it to the other side, unscathed, and shitless. You may get some bumps and cuts along the way, but for the most part, you will have an easier time keeping yourself safe from impact.

On an emotional level, this teaches you that your needs are valuable, that you are safe within yourself, and that you do not need to seek validation, support, and protection from others. Because you are self-validated, and see and honor your own value, you can begin to attract positive people into your life who are going to have the capacity to offer you high-quality, stress-free relationships.

Something To Think About

1. Are you being true to yourself in all of your relationships?

2. Are your emotional needs being met in all of your relationships?

3. Do you have effective communication in all of your relationships?

4. Are you confident speaking up for what you need in all of your relationships?

5. Are there any relationships in your life that cause you more anxiety than happiness?

6. If this relationship is worth salvaging, what steps will you take to salvage it so that it better satisfies your emotional needs? If this relationship is not worth salvaging, what steps will you take to end it?

CHAPTER 10

POOR THINKING HABITS

IF A POOR RELATIONSHIP can shit all over your mood and leave you feeling anxious and messy, imagine what negative thinking can do to you. When we engage in negative thinking, we are basically engaging in a low-quality relationship with ourselves, which can lead to all of the same complications. Except, with ourselves, there is no escaping, so we basically *have* to get our ducks in a row and figure our nonsense out so that we can start loving ourselves more and living in mental peace.

When you engage in a low-quality relationship with yourself, it can be a sign that negative thinking and pessimism are in some way influential in the way you see the world. You may find yourself constantly judging and criticizing yourself, and likely doing the same to others and the world around you. As a matter of fact, if you want to stop judging yourself so much, the secret is to stop judging others.

Judgmental behavior is not compartmentalized, so if you're really hard on other people and look down on them, you'll also be really hard on yourself and look down on yourself. This constant negativity leads you to feel like you suck, everyone sucks, everything sucks, and nothing will ever change to not suck. Who wants to live an existence where they have no capacity to experience anything desirable?

The more you entertain these negative thinking tendencies, the more anxious you are going to feel. Surely, you can see how living a hopeless existence in a hopeless world could make you a little anxious. And here's the other kicker—most people who think extremely negatively tend to believe that everyone else thinks this way, too, which means that not only are you harshly judging yourself but you are also assuming that everyone else is, too. This means that, in your mind, you are failing to live up to your own expectations and the expectations of every other person around you.

Fortunately for you, most people do not give one tenth of a shit about who you are or what you do because they're too busy being self-conscious and worrying about what you think of them, so all of the judgment that you are experiencing is really coming from within yourself and toward yourself. This sounds silly, and in many ways, it is. The good thing, however, is that you can begin to own the fact that the only person judging you so harshly is you, which means that you can correct your own behaviors and change your experience.

But where is this negativity coming from? Obviously, it is coming from the fact that you seem to have nothing nice to say about yourself and apparently that saying your mother repeated over and over about how "*If you don't have anything nice to say, don't say anything at all*" didn't stick. However, it is likely also coming from the fact that you are a human, and humans are equipped with this little survival tool that psychologists call "negativity bias." Negativity bias is the name for the convenient little tool our brain uses which causes us to think negatively about things all the time so that we can prevent ourselves from getting hurt.

By remaining skeptical and negative about everything, we can avoid and deny the things that hurt us in the past or that we believe may hurt us in the future. This way, we cannot actually get hurt. Really, back when we were cave people this was a valuable tool because we could identify our need to stay away from dangerous animals and falling debris. Sure, the kitty might *look* cute and fuzzy, but the fact that it's littermate just ripped a gazelle to shreds, leaving only the bones, in less than 10 minutes flat means it's probably dangerous. See, negativity bias could be lifesaving.

Of course, it does still have many uses in the modern world. Thanks to negativity bias, you know that it is not a good idea to touch anything too hot, to stick your fingers under a moving blade, to step in front of a moving vehicle, or to otherwise engage in a behavior that may leave you seriously injured or seriously deceased. However, our minds have grown so powerful and intricate that our negativity bias can also become a serious pain in the you-know-what, too.

For example, when you think that a person laughing 20 feet away from you is laughing at how dumb you look, or when you think that playing intramural frisbee is going to get out of hand and result in your demise, you're experiencing modern day, unnecessary negativity bias. See, while these are possibilities, the chances are highly unlikely, which means that you needn't be so anxious about it. Still, thanks to your prehistoric brain being lazy, you keep believing that the sky is falling, everything bad is happening to you and that there is absolutely nothing good worth living for.

Most people stay in the pattern of negativity bias because they have no idea what it is or how they can get out of it in the first place. And they've never stopped to think about the default settings of their thoughts. As a result, they find themselves feeling trapped in this pessimistic mindset that keeps throwing them through loops of stress, worry, and anxiety. Understanding your negativity bias and recognizing that this is a natural process in your brain can help you detach from the belief that your negativity is a part of your personal identity so that you can begin allowing yourself to welcome in new, more positive elements of your identity. Not to mention, it will give the awareness and perspective to recognize when you're experiencing irrational fears. So you can observe your negativity bias, label it, and release it.

As you continually begin identifying negativity bias for

what it is, then overcoming your mental laziness so that you can actually increase your inner potential and overcome your poor thinking habits becomes a lot easier. You will find yourself no longer being attached to your negative thoughts and instead replacing that space with new, positive thoughts. Through this, you will feel a lot less anxious because you will no longer be convinced that the big bad wolf is coming to get you. Your brain, then, can relax and stop looking for every reason to be afraid, concerned, or on guard for its own protection. You can overcome your natural evolution and evolve into a positive thinking, level-headed, anxiety-free superhuman.

Something To Think About

1. In what ways do you judge others?
2. Do those ways have overlap with the ways that you judge yourself?
3. What are the most common fears you have around what people think about you?
4. What was a time that you thought or assumed someone had a negative opinion about you, but it turned out not to be true?

CHAPTER 11

LEARNED BEHAVIOR

PREPARE YOUR "THANK YOU" speech for your parents and your odd babysitter once again, as we are about to dive into another way that your childhood could have effed you up—I mean, adversely played a role in your tendency to be an anxious person. As we know, personality can be shaped by the people around us and the circumstances that we encounter, which can make behaving anxiously the product of us having certain personality traits that make us more prone to anxiety. But sometimes, the answer is not nearly as complex as a full-fledged personality shift. Sometimes, the reason why you are anxious is that you watched someone in your childhood behave anxiously, and now, you are experiencing anxiety as a result of this learned behavior.

That's right. There are people out there, perhaps yourself included, who have anxiety solely because they watched other people behave anxiously and picked up on it. When this happens, your body engages in a process called biofeedback, which stimulates anxiety based on the physical behaviors that you are engaging in.

So, say your Mom was a particularly anxious person, and she always fidgeted when she was waiting in line as a way to attempt to cope with her anxiety. Even if you were not personally anxious, you might have seen this and picked up on it as being normal behavior, thus causing you to start fidgeting when you are waiting in lines, too.

As a result of biofeedback, your brain recognizes you physically responding to your environment in a way that typically indicates that you are anxious, which causes it to start developing anxious reactions. Through this, you can begin experiencing physical and mental symptoms of anxiety which, if you engage in this behavior often enough, can genuinely seem as though they belong to you personally.

If you grew up with someone with anxiety, especially if you were around them frequently from birth to age seven, you need to consider that your anxiety may be a learned trait rather than an organic one that you developed yourself. Why age seven, you ask? From the time that we are born until we reach seven years old, we are constantly absorbing everything around us, as we are essentially learning how to be humans. During this time, we are extra attentive to people's body language, behavior, words, how they engage with other people, their feelings, their beliefs, their values, and everything else.

We tend to pick up the most from our parents, or anyone

who we are spending a significant amount of time around, so pay close attention to these people. If you're screwed in the head, it's probably their fault. Recall if you spent any time around anyone who was consistently nervous, or portraying signs of high stress or nervousness. Pay close attention to how you were in response to these individuals as well, because sometimes we do not directly copy their behaviors, but instead learn to be anxious or nervous in response to their behavior. For example, if you had an emotionally volatile parent, you may find yourself anxious any time you are around emotionally volatile people or even emotionally normal people who are experiencing intense emotional responses in a natural and healthy manner.

Giving yourself the opportunity to understand and identify where in your childhood you may have been influenced to behave in an anxious manner can help you understand why you may be having these responses now. Once you can understand these natural responses, you will be inclined to have a deeper sense of understanding and compassion toward yourself anytime you are in a situation where your anxiety begins to spike.

Finding out that your anxiety comes from childhood, specifically with learned behaviors, can actually be a blessing in disguise as this is often one of the easiest types of anxiety that you can overcome. These behaviors, once identified, can be recognized as not belonging to you, which means that you can release them and recognize that they were never yours in the first place.

Imagine your learned anxiety to be some dirty gym socks that your workout buddy slipped into your bag by mistake, and you took them home. You can either allow those stinky socks to follow you through life and make everything rancid and worse, or you can realize they're not yours, and give them right back to your workout buddy and say, "No thanks, bucko!" Or you could say something in a way that's not so nice, but the general idea remains.

You can do the same thing with your anxious behaviors, even if it has been years since you learned them and began expressing them yourself in your own life. No, you don't have to literally go to your mom's house, storm in after your epiphany, and yell "Here's your lip twitch back! No thanks, bucko!" But the more you begin to identify that certain behaviors are not your own, the more of your anxiety you can "give back" so to speak to their rightful owners and move on with your life.

The hippie folk of the world believe that we all have an "inner child" that continues to recall all of the experiences we have ever had in life, good or bad. Normal folk call this "memory." When you engage in the "woo woo" method of healing this, you visualize yourself going back into your childhood self and telling yourself that you no longer need to carry this anxiety with you because it does not belong to you and it does not serve you. When you engage in the normal method, you simply go back into your memories, acknowledge what you did not understand back then, and re-teach yourself new information based on what is actually the truth.

Really, you can use whatever method is going to work for you to help you go back into your memory bank and undo the beliefs you had at that time that lead to you taking on other people's behaviors in the first place. If you want to hold a ceremony, light some candles, and do it the woo woo way because it's the fastest way for you to become anxiety-free, do engage your weird little heart in whatever feels right for you. If you want to just get a notebook and a pen, and simply revisit your memories, then re-educate and re-program yourself on what the truth is with the new information you have now, do that. Whatever helps you chill out, bro.

Something To Think About

1. Is there anyone from your past that you think behaves in anxious ways or has anxious tendencies?
2. Has this person rubbed off on you in any way?
3. Is there anyone from your present that you think behaves in anxious ways or has anxious tendencies?
4. Has this person rubbed off on you in any way?

PART 3

CHANGING WHAT'S IN YOUR CONTROL

CHAPTER 12

YOU ARE NOT A PURPLE DONKEY

YOU ARE NOT A PURPLE DONKEY. That's what I've had to tell myself over and over again since…the incident in 2nd grade. Let's be honest: you've probably encountered a fair amount of douchebags in your life who have said some just plain douchy shit to you, am I right? For me, it was that guy that found out I had a crush on him and said he would never like a girl with my elephant ears. And that teacher who said in front of the whole Math class that I couldn't handle an honors class. No one has ever actually called me a purple donkey, but the words don't matter. The point is that sometimes we start to believe and give power to the words that people say about us, no matter how ridiculous or negative they may be.

Virtually all of us have been bullied in one way or another, and many of us continue to hold on to what those people said when they bullied us because, well, it hurt. Also, if it happened before that magical age of seven, we may have deeply internalized it and identified with it because that is simply how our strange little brains work.

That being said, you need to learn how to tune out the douches, and stop allowing their words to be so powerful. Determining your self-worth and making your life decisions now based on something some idiot with pencils in his nose said to you on a school bus fifteen years ago isn't exactly going to set you up for having a good life. And it's not going to help you to stop having random meltdowns every time something in your life triggers this unpleasant memory.

Learning how to practice self-validation ultimately comes down to you learning how to stop giving a crap about what everyone else says to you and start giving more focus to what you feel about yourself. You have to give your opinion of yourself more value than someone else's opinion of you. You need to trust the way you see yourself more than you trust the way other people see you. This can often come down to trusting yourself and valuing your opinion in general, even when it doesn't come to your own personal self-image.

In fact, if you are the type of person who hates or fears making decisions, who doesn't trust your decisions in general, and who would rather someone else make choices for you than you make them yourself, chances are that sentiment bleeds over into your self-image. If you value someone else's ability to choose over your own, chances are you also value someone else's opinion over your own when it comes to how you see yourself. The two are interconnected.

So the more you can learn to validate yourself, the easier it is going to be for you to stop concerning yourself with everyone else and feeling down every time people have an opinion about you that hurts your feelings. When mama said *If you don't have anything nice to say, don't say anything at all*, not everyone got the memo, so it's going to be up to you to have the self-confidence and self-assurance to validate yourself even when other people are not validating you. As a result, you'll find yourself experiencing less anxiety whenever people are treating you in a way that would have previously triggered you, such as by belittling you or invalidating your emotions or opinions.

In a sense, learning to validate yourself now is a way for you to stand up to those douchebags from your past so that you can stop allowing yourself to continually be dragged down by them even long after they have forgotten about you. While you're always stammering around attractive people and suffering through low quality relationships as a result of your diminished self-esteem because idiot Bobby with the pencils in his nose called you ugly in 6th grade, idiot Bobby is now off yachting in Sardinia with his Russian supermodel wife, counting his money from his multi-million dollar pencil empire...possibly still with pencils in his nose, but he's off living his best life while you're here living your worst.

So let this be your way of digging yourself back out of the

hole that you let yourself be tossed in when the bullies of the past did what bullies do, and you let them set up shop in your head, rent-free. Now, instead of letting their voices haunt you and alter your beliefs about yourself, you can let yourself be freed from their opinions of you, and instead grow into your own.

Self-validation is something that some people learn how to do early on, but not all of us are taught this behavior. The easiest way to tell if you're lacking in the self-validation department is to pause for a moment and look at the immediate influences around you. These are the people who can rub off on your psyche in either a negative or positive way. Ask yourself what type of people you are surrounding yourself with, and how you respond to people who do not treat you kindly.

Are you surrounding yourself with people who genuinely care about you? Or are you surrounding yourself with people who are just overall shitty people? In other words, do your friends accept you and support you? Or do they make you feel like a complete idiot when you're voicing your opinion and it happens to differ from theirs? If you told them you wanted to quit your finance job, grow a beard, and move to an alpaca farm to play ukulele all day and live a more peaceful existence, how would they respond?

This is not about your friends having to agree with you all the time to be good friends, but if your friends treat you like you're an idiot and like your thoughts and opinions are stupid, this points to signs that you may have surrounded yourself with people who do not treat you respectfully. Yes, I know, the goal is *self*-validation, but it's also important to make sure you're not unnecessarily exposing yourself to people who can tarnish your self-worth and put a damper on the way you feel. So look at the people around you, evaluate their behaviors, and critically consider whether or not these are good people who really deserve a spot in your squad.

One potential outcome of this evaluation is that upon closer inspection, it is confirmed that they do indeed suck, and you need to drop them like a hot brick as fast as you can. The other potential outcome of this is to look at their behaviors and realize that they do actually treat you respectfully and you are taking things too personally and misinterpreting many of their behaviors as being invalidating. At this point, it's time to look in the mirror.

Are you being oversensitive and shriveling up every single time someone does not agree with you or accidentally doesn't hear you when you are sharing something with them? Do you instantly jump to the conclusion that you are being ignored or punished for having your own thoughts, beliefs, or opinions? What are your natural responses, and are they healthy and sensible given the situation you are in or are they excessive and habitual based on how you have been treated in past relationships?

At first, it can be hard to determine whether your responses are valid responses to harsh people or excessive responses to typical people. You may find yourself questioning whether you are crazy, or they are crazy, and this is completely normal. You will find in time that as you continue to look objectively at the relationships you share with people, it becomes easier for you to see what is truly going on and how you need to respond to the situations that you are a part of. If you are being treated poorly by people, you know that you will need to adjust or eliminate these relationships to support your own mental health and wellbeing. If you're just extra and have disproportionate freak outs in the midst of every conversation or small disagreement because of your own insecurity, you need to adjust your own responses so that you can stop feeling overwhelmed by everyone in your life.

Aside from paying attention to how and where the responses are coming from, you also need to start validating yourself. You are going to need to validate yourself in either situation: whether you need to end a relationship or simply adjust the way you show up in a relationship, so learning some basic self-validation techniques is vital and necessary if you are going to go on to have healthy relationships in your life. So let's get into a little bit of how-to.

Be Present With Yourself

One way to start validating yourself is to be present with yourself in life so that you can begin identifying what it feels like to just be with you, and tune in to your own mind and thoughts. In many cases, in a moment of anxiety, people will immediately start looking around at everyone else's behaviors, actions, and thoughts to start formulating an opinion about what is going on and what they should do. This can lead to you having a habit of looking outside of yourself to see if what you are feeling is valid or reasonable, which can create a lack of trust and compassion toward yourself.

Although looking around at others is a great way to evaluate any situation from a logical standpoint, looking at other people to the point of no longer considering your own opinions and feelings can lead you to always trusting other people more than yourself, which can leave you vulnerable to taking on other people's unkind or unfair thoughts and opinions about you.

Being present with yourself can sound like some strange woo woo stuff, but I mean, in reality, you can't escape yourself so you might as well accept that and learn to make the best of it. All it really means is that you need to look inward at your own thoughts, feelings, and opinions and incorporate them as a more significant part of your evaluations of situations than the thoughts, feelings, and opinions of others. When we don't take the time to become aware of what we are experiencing, we naturally completely overlook our own experience, which keeps us feeling more anxious.

If you sit and listen to yourself, you may find that you were feeling uncomfortable about something small, but because you failed to acknowledge that there was discomfort within you, it grew. Think about it like a tiny stuffed animal sitting in a doorway casting a massive shadow on the wall, and you are a young innocent child lying in bed freaking out about the shadow on the wall. Had you stopped to pay attention to where the shadow was coming from, it wouldn't be so scary, but because you didn't, instead you wet your bed because you thought a monster was coming to eat you.

Accurately Identify Your Thoughts, Feelings, And Opinions

Oftentimes, our emotions are simply small reminders that we have needs or desires, and they help keep us on track with having those needs or desires met. For example, say you begin feeling anxiety because you are angry with a certain person and you are fearful that your next encounter will turn into a confrontation, and you are fearful of emotional confrontations. Acknowledging and accurately identifying your anger and fear can support you in deciding what an effective solution for those feelings would be. Perhaps instead of going in unprepared, you may decide ahead of time what it is that you want to say and how you want to handle the situation so that your emotions do not take over when you are talking with your friend.

In some cases, you do not even need to act on your emotions, but just need to simply observe them and sit with them. Yeah, sometimes chilling out means doing just that: identifying your emotions and then letting yourself chill the frick out so they do not continue to fester.

The key here is to take an objective stance so you can actually be clear on what it is that you are experiencing, and choose how to proceed accordingly.

So when you find yourself in a moment of anxiety, ask yourself:

- What am I feeling in this moment?
- Is that feeling happening in proportion to what is actually going on?
- What am I truly afraid of in this moment?
- Is that feared outcome a life or death situation?
- Is it reversible or fixable?
- How likely is the feared worst case scenario to actually happen?

This will help you look at things from a more objective point of view and accurately identify what is actually going on so you can mitigate an anxious response.

Normalize Your Experience

Normalizing what you experience is necessary when it comes to self-validation. Oftentimes, people search for outside validation because they think the response they are having to a situation is unreasonable or abnormal, which leads to them feeling like they are silly. If you genuinely believe that you are having excessive or irrational emotional responses to your life experiences (and people that you trust and who genuinely care about you agree), you may benefit from looking deeper to get a handle on what is going on. In this situation, a therapist may help, as chances are, you have something under the hood that needs a more serious inspection.

However, if you are simply worried about your emotions

in general, realize that whatever you are feeling in response to what you are going through is likely natural. Realize that even if other people do not have the exact same reaction as you to every situation, it doesn't mean you are abnormal, as each and every person comes into situations with their own unique baggage. It's more about the level of your reactions and emotions being a signal that things are out of hand, rather than the specific reactions themselves. But don't allow the fact that you're being triggered to make you anxious.

Having an emotional response to something is perfectly normal. Don't forget that. You're not doing anything wrong or unreasonable by having an emotional response to what you are going through. Believe it or not, we are not all the iron clad soldiers that society has taught us that we are supposed to be. You are not a wimp. You are a human. And it is okay to be a mere human.

CHAPTER 13

WHAT'S UP WITH THE LENS?

WE ALL HAVE a lens that we view life through. We can call that lens, perspective. Everyone's lens has been shaped and shaded differently by their unique, individual life experiences, which means that everyone sees life through a different perspective. This means two things: you cannot see things exactly the way other people do, and they cannot see things exactly the way you do. It also means that if you do not like what you are looking at, you need to change the lens and start looking at something more appealing.

Shifting your perspective does not always need to equal you polishing a turd and calling it gold, despite the fact that it can feel that way when someone gives you that kind of advice. In fact, in many cases, something big and ugly about your life may continue to look big and ugly no matter what way you look at it. This is normal. And this is okay. Instead of allowing yourself to feel like a complete failure because you could not alchemize shit into gold, you can allow yourself to pull your perspective back and start putting it in alignment with the bigger picture.

Sometimes, a birds' eye perspective will not help polish the turd, but it will help you see that the turd is fairly minimal in relation to everything else in your life. In fact, when you look at the bigger picture, you may realize that most things are actually completely meaningless in your life and that your perspective was making them (and you) seem far more important than they actually are. Feeling inspired yet?

That being said, poor perspective can keep you thinking that this turd is an impassible mountain that is going to hold you hostage and hold a dark, stinky cloud over your head for the rest of your life. When you have poor perspective, oftentimes you will only see things that are challenging or negative, which can keep you feeling like the world is a scary place. Instead of seeing the entirety of reality, you focus on things like your scary shadow, what that person really meant when they said that one thing, and how you came across when you behaved that weird way at lunch. As you may have picked up on, you look at life through the lens of your negativity bias and, as a result, everything about the world seems big and scary and negative.

Perspective should be used as a tool to help you heal, not to help you avoid. Many people will turn a blind eye toward something painful because they are afraid of facing it and dealing with that pain. The reality is, there is no reason for you to have to ignore something in your world simply because you do not like the way it looks.

Not only is it rude, but it is also ineffective and will lead to you dropping another load of crap into your baggage, making life even harder for you in the long run. Instead of trying to ignore the pile of crap that you are afraid of acknowledging, start learning how to see it from a different perspective. Who knows, maybe if you change the lens enough times you'll realize there was something amazing buried under that pile of shit of yours.

Identify Your Reactive Perspective

When it comes to shifting your perspective, the first thing that you need to do is get clear on what you are actually looking at. After all, it can be challenging to shift anything if you are unwilling to become aware of it and get clear on what it is and what needs to be done. The first step here is going to be to identify what your natural perspective is, and what your reactive perspective is when it comes to discovering what your reaction to people is.

Your reactive perspective is going to be how you shift your perspective based on what triggers have happened in your environment. For example, you might feel confident and positive in general, but if someone criticizes you, you immediately begin to feel negative and unconfident. If this is the case, you know that your reactive perspective is one that is not serving you, and you need to begin shifting it so that you can stop wavering based on what other people think or say. Self-validation will come into play here, so you're not putting on someone else's lens rather than seeing through your own. Ever put on someone else's glasses and gotten an instantaneous migraine, acquired a severed eye-ache, you suddenly couldn't see anything right, and the room started spinning? Yeah, don't do that.

When you are getting a feel for what your knee-jerk reactions to things are, make sure that you are very honest with yourself. Sometimes, it can be embarrassing to admit that we are a basket full of negative that is raining all over our own parade, which can make it hard to own everything that we are projecting into our world. That being said, being brutally honest about where exactly you are on the Debbie Downer scale really is necessary for you to see what needs to change and then start implementing changes that will actually affect positive changes in your world.

Put It Into Perspective

Once you have thoroughly disappointed yourself with acknowledging how negative you actually are, you want to start paying attention to how your negativities can be changed. The best way to begin this process is to focus on where you are unreasonable with your perspective and start shifting that, as oftentimes, we have unreasonable perspectives that are completely unfounded. In other words, you have totally been lying to yourself—so if you ever thought you were a bad liar, think again! You have likely been lying to yourself for years about the magnitude of things in your life and whether or not they are actually as bad as they seem. In reality, they are not, but you have lied your way into believing that they are.

So look at what is in front of you and decide whether or not you are a total drama queen about it. Just like we mentioned earlier with your relationships, look at the situation at hand, and start by acknowledging how you are feeling about it and what opinions you have in reaction to the information or situation. Then ask yourself if perhaps you are having an excessive response to the situation at hand. It is important for you to pay attention to what you are actually going through and whether or not you perceive it in an honest way. Sometimes, especially when we are dealing with anxiety, we have a tendency to distort our vision and believe that everything we are looking at is out to get us and that we are doomed to have a terrible life forever and ever.

So try zooming out and seeing the bigger picture. At the end of the day, does it really even matter if that person saw you trip on the sidewalk? Do you really think you'll always remember that one time you said something silly and someone looked at you like you were off your rocker?

Remember when you were a kid and you'd come home crying to your mom about how your crush pointed and laughed at you because you came out of the bathroom with toilet paper under your shoe? You went on and on about how they were the love of your life and now your life is ruined for good and you'll never find anyone again as amazing as they were so you're doomed to a loveless life of misery and you can never leave the house or show your face again, and you burst into the ugly cry and nearly drowned in your own tears. And your mom placed her

hand on your shoulder, took one look at you in the eyes...
and laughed.

Things may bother you in the moment, and they may even
bother you for a while, but as the situation gets further in
the past, it becomes easier for you to stop worrying so
much about it. Eventually, you forget, and the incident
means nothing to you anymore. In most cases, the only
reason it even mattered in the first place was because of
your anxiety, and not because it was actually a significant
incident.

So zoom out, and look at things honestly. If after zooming
out, you find that the situation is still significant and will
impact you in a big way, you are going to want to choose
how to look at it from that point forward. Typically, you
have two choices: you can look at it as though it is in
control over you and you can do nothing about it, or you
can look at it as a lesson that you can somehow learn or
grow from.

Say the love of your life leaves you, and the relationship
that you adored is now over. Naturally, you will grieve
through the process of losing someone you loved, but even
as you grieve, you can still choose to keep everything in
perspective. For one, you can choose to see this as the end
and believe that there is no possible way that you could
move forward and your life is now essentially over—or on
the other hand, you can see it as a painful situation that
you will learn and grow from so you can be better in your
next relationship with the right person.

If you choose the former perspective, you are going to

experience excessive amounts of despair, grief, guilt, frustration, disappointment, stress, and anxiety. If you choose the latter, you will still hurt and grieve for a time, but you will also see that it was a beautiful experience while it lasted and that you will go on to have more beautiful experiences again in your future once you are done grieving. It is entirely up to you which perspective you choose to use.

Reframe And Own Your Perspective

Once you have put everything into perspective, you need to officially choose what perspective you want to have on things and then own that perspective. In the last example, we said you need to choose how you are going to look at things. The next step, though, is to own it and stick with it. That's right—owning your perspective essentially means that you are making a decision to see something a certain way and that you are now maintaining that decision. This takes you out of a state of indecisiveness so that you do not go back and forth like a confused lab rat trying to find the cheese in the ridiculous maze you have been trapped inside of. Instead, make your decision, stick with it, and see it through. Owning your perspective can be done best by first doing the work of finding the perspective that is most honest and fitting, and then choosing to maintain that perspective from that point forward.

It is important to understand that owning your perspective does not mean that you shift into a closed-minded state of existence. You are not necessarily going to exist in your decision without ever being willing to see new information that may present itself to you that could allow you to make a better decision from that point. Instead, owning your perspective means that for now, you have looked at all of the information presented and available to you in this moment, and you have chosen to see things a certain way, a better way. Should you be presented with new relevant information in the future, you may revisit your perspective —but in the meantime, you are choosing to maintain this one. The purpose for this is that you act from a place of decisiveness and clarity, while still maintaining an open mind should you ever need to shift your perspective again.

CHAPTER 14

DUDE, JUST LET IT GO

INCOMPLETE EMOTIONS CAN LEAD to a whirlpool of drama inside of us when we are not careful, and that drama can quickly escalate into ongoing anxiety. Many people believe that once the urge to stop expressing an emotion disappears, the emotion itself has been dealt with, but that is not always the case. Our brains can be experts at sweeping emotions right under the rug and then falling into inner turmoil later on when we realize that those emotions are still there. Think of them as your adulthood boogie monster, hiding under the bed, waiting to creep out and give you a mental breakdown at any given moment without warning. Getting stuck behind your emotions can be stressful and overwhelming, making it more likely for you to experience ongoing anxiety for a long period of time.

When you do not express your emotions on purpose, they will sit in your body in an incomplete cycle, which means that they will find inopportune times to rear up. For example, say your ex-lover said something cruel to you, and you felt hurt but wanted to save face, so you did not cry or do anything to express how hurt you felt. Years later, in a newer relationship, if your partner said something nice to you, you might find yourself bubbling over with tears and sadness because you recall what it felt like to be invalidated and treated poorly by your ex. Now, your new lover is wondering why you cannot take a compliment, you have to explain your story of your ex-lover's cruelty, and the whole situation feels painful and uncomfortable.

Of course, this is all a part of the healing process—and if your new lover is not a douchebag, they will understand and sit with you through the process as you heal your emotions. Still, it can be uncomfortable and frustrating to have feelings rearing up from months or even years ago, especially when logically you believe they should be complete because so much time has passed. As it turns out, they lied—time does not heal everything. It is what you choose to do in that time that determines whether or not you are actually going to heal from everything you have been through.

Holding onto things negatively impacts you by filling up your emotional bottle with several different unexpressed emotions and creating the opportunity for you to experience extreme overwhelm. Just one unexpressed emotion can lead to a strange and out of place emotional reaction to various situations in your life if you are not careful because unexpressed emotions can wreak havoc in the body. For that reason, you can likely imagine how overwhelming weeks, months, or even years of unexpressed emotions can wreak havoc on you.

Many people are unaware of what they are holding on to, or the fact that they are holding on to anything at all because they believe that they can simply ignore unwanted emotions and they will go away. Of course, this is not true. Emotions are not to be treated as an unwanted house-guest that does not seem to get the hint that they are unwelcome and need to leave the premises immediately. Emotions are a part of you, and they are a necessary biological function that was designed to help you navigate life as a human. Attempting to deny them essentially tells your brain that you are going to act in spite of what it is telling you, which amplifies your stress because it leaves your brain feeling like you are in danger. So the more emotions you hold on to, the more your body will continue to feel that you are in danger.

Over time, not expressing your emotions or failing to let things go can result in the development of things like anger, anxiety, and depression. In this specific circumstance, these responses are the result of your inability to truly let things go, which means that you are experiencing anger, anxiety, or depression as a secondary emotion.

In a sense, the first emotion festered so much that now, you are experiencing an even greater and more complex emotional response because your body is desperately trying to get your attention so that you can heal what is going on inside of you. Of course, until now, you have likely been stubbornly ignoring your body's and mind's pleas. But if you are ready to stop experiencing anger, anxiety, and depression as a secondary response to unexpressed emotions, you need to start working through letting things go so that you can release all of the suppressed emotions around your experiences.

The Types Of Things You Are Holding On To

As humans, we hold on to all kinds of different things. We are sometimes like delicate little sponges. A sponge can't pick and choose what it absorbs—it just soaks everything up and finds itself full of a weird gross mixture of all kinds of things it wants nothing to do with. And once it's full, it doesn't have room to take on anything else, even if it's something good. And that's how we can be as humans if we're not careful.

Chances are, you're holding on to a lot of different things, ranging from regular old memories to traumatic experiences. Sometimes, what we are holding on to is no longer within our cognitive awareness, meaning that we cannot pull it back up as a memory, but emotionally, we still remember it and hold on to it like it just happened. We also tend to hold on to hopes, dreams, failures, and losses. Essentially, anything that creates a deep emotional response within us, whether we realize it or not, will be held on to within us so that we can hopefully eventually sort through it and close the cycle.

And what is the source of all this? It could be possible that you are holding on to the emotions that stem from a specific experience that you had in life. Even if you cannot fully place the memory, you may have small ideas of what happened to you that caused you to have such an intense emotional reaction to what you were going through. It is important that as you dive into these past experiences, you don't judge yourself or feel disappointed in yourself or embarrassed about what happened or how you felt. Judging yourself for feeling bad about how you felt bad about an experience isn't really helping.

It is also possible that underneath the surface, you have many bad experiences or memories all relating to one original memory. For example, let's say in middle school, someone called you fat. That one experience was painful, but you might have gone on to have a series of problematic experiences stemming from that original source of pain that made you believe that you were too fat. Maybe you belittled yourself, denied yourself your grandma's favorite family recipe, were self-conscious when eating on dates, never felt comfortable while working out in public, or a whole slew of other instances where you altered your behavior or feelings about yourself to be in line with a mean remark that was once said to you.

If something like this sounds familiar, and you have negative emotions from multiple bad experiences, you'll need to work through and release every single new memory and hurt, as simply releasing the first one is unfortunately not the cheat code for healing everything that came after it. Take your time and be gentle with yourself. In the interest of you being your best self and living your best life, even if your emotional reaction was warranted for the situation, for your own sake, dude, you really need to just let it go.

Don't Add To The Damage

Now that you have convinced yourself that you need to let go of what no longer serves you, there are two ways of doing this: consciously choosing to let go of the memories, and working through the remaining emotions that came as a result. In a sense, you are doing what should have been done immediately after the memory took place, but you can do it now in retrospect. Realize, however, that it may come with added emotions now that you have spent so long repressing it. You may also begin to feel feelings of betrayal or abandonment from your own prior unwillingness to sit with yourself. Again, do not judge yourself, simply allow these things to bubble up to the surface, and feel your way through them.

At this point, you are going to have to be careful that you express your feelings in a healthy way so that you do not re-traumatize yourself or give yourself a deeper reason to hide your emotions from yourself if they feel too painful or overwhelming. Learning how to express your emotions in a healthy manner shows you that you can feel emotions without having such intense responses or negative consequences, and that you can in fact have a healthy resolve.

The goal is to feel positive about releasing your feelings so you'll feel a complete and satisfying sense of release without harboring shame or guilt for your expressions having adverse consequences. For example, if you were angry and you were processing residual anger, calling your Dad and blowing up on him for how he treated you twenty years ago is probably just going to make you feel unstable and guilty that you called him and hurt his feelings over the phone, seemingly out of the blue. As a result, you are only going to deepen the pain, not lessen it.

Practice The Art Of Detachment

In addition to letting go of everything that you have been holding on to in the past, you also need to start letting go of everything that happens in the present. After all, emptying out your emotional reservoir only to refill it with new emotional turmoil is only going to lead to you feeling like you are right back where you started. Learning how to engage in detachment in the present is a great opportunity for you to let go of everything that you would have been likely to hold on to so that you can begin feeling better right away. Instead of sticking a needle in your eye, then trying to remove it, you could just...not stick the needle in your eye. Doesn't that sound more pleasant?

Detachment is taught in many different ways, but at the root of it is learning how to accept things as they are in the moment. When you engage in the art of detachment, you release your attachment to certain expectations or outcomes so that you are more accepting of whatever happens. This way, because you were never attached to a specific outcome or experience in the first place, it is much easier for you to be okay, no matter what happens.

To be clear, this is not about releasing all standards for yourself and your life and resigning to the fact that everything will just have to stay in shambles because you don't want to ever run the risk of being disappointed. This is not an excuse to be lazy. Healthy detachment is about having a clear set of goals and desires, doing everything in your power to ensure your desired outcome, yet being willing to allow things to unfold as they will, which means that you are open to the possibility of change or unexpected experiences, knowing that no matter what, you'll be alright.

This requires you to loosen your grips on your expectations. It is as simple as realizing that you do not have a crystal ball, you are not Miss Cleo, and you're not the big guy upstairs. You cannot predict outcomes, and you are not able to control everything. While you can (and should) have hopes, know that it is not a guarantee that everything you want will happen exactly how you want, when you want, where you want, and with whom you want. So that means that I just have to accept the fact that I may not get a marriage proposal on the evening of my birthday under a shooting star in Paris, from Leonardo DiCaprio.

When you're too attached to your hopes, they become expectations, and when these expectations are not fulfilled to your idea of perfection, they become feelings of hurt. You may begin to doubt yourself, resent yourself or others, or feel disappointed or annoyed with life because you are not getting what you wanted. When this happens frequently, you may find yourself anxious.

Most people feel like the tighter you hold on to your

expectations, the more likely they are to happen, yet the opposite is usually the truth. The harder you try to force something into place, the less likely it will be that said thing actually turns into what you hoped it would. Instead, you will likely fight so hard and desperately for it that you end up forcing it in the opposite direction. Have you ever wanted so desperately to make a good impression on someone that you ended up completely in your head and making a fool of yourself?

Here's a tip when it comes to goals. Have them. Have outcome goals, but more importantly, have *action* goals. Your actions are the things you can control 100%. So make action goals that require you to take relevant actions towards what you ultimately want, and judge yourself based on whether you are taking consistent action or not like you said you would.

For example, if your goal is to get into a relationship and get a new boyfriend or girlfriend, that is an outcome goal— to be boo'd up. Once you set that in your mind, forget about it and focus on consistently doing the things that will eventually get you there. Make a profile on all the online dating apps and spend 10 minutes a day chatting with potential suitors. Start a conversation with a stranger at Starbucks every morning when you get your morning coffee. Go to the weekly speed-dating event every Saturday. If your goal is to become a multi-million dollar real estate agent, cool. Set it in your mind, but forget about it and focus on generating 10 new qualified leads a day.

So instead of having anxiety over the fact that you're not

yet a multi-millionaire married to Leonardo DiCaprio, you can have peace in knowing that you are steadily doing what it takes to progressively get there. Forget about the outcome goal, but just keep taking action toward it. If you do that, it is inevitable for you to reach your desired outcome, or something even better before you know it.

Absolute-ly...Nothing

Part of learning how to detach from your expectations and desires is learning how to stay open to all possibilities. This means that you are willing to see things from a different point of view and that you are willing to experience different outcomes that are not always what you expected they would be. This way, when things do not go as planned, you can still find peace in the outcome and feel happy with what you have experienced, as you continue to look for the good in everything.

This can be accomplished with a single mindset shift: removing the belief in absolutes. When you remove absolutes from your mind, you essentially stop guaranteeing outcomes to yourself, whether good or bad. So, stop saying things like "I am absolutely going to get that promotion if I do this one thing," or "I am absolutely going to fall flat on my face if I try to walk over and talk to that person." This way, you don't set yourself up for emotional failure. Being open to things happening differently, can also incite an exciting feeling of curiosity. You hate it when people spoil movie endings for you, right? You want the excitement of seeing for yourself how it all turns out.

When you are open and curious in situations that you are convinced will go poorly, you can instead be in the mindset of wanting to learn more and wondering what will come of it. This way, you no longer feel like you have to be excellent at something, such as an excellent fit for a new friendship or excellent at a new hobby. There's no pressure, you're open and curious, you're just exploring new things. If it goes as you hoped it would, that's great. However, if it does not, you will find that you are still able to remain calm and confident anyway and you'll have the mental and emotional maturity to simply try a different route in the future until you get a desirable outcome, rather than shutting yourself off.

In situations where you are confident that something will go well, and things go left, staying open and curious means that you will continue to stay open even if things do not go as planned. This way, if you felt confident that you would get something like a promotion or a certain response from someone in your life and you don't, you do not feel like a big fat loser when it does not happen. Instead, you are able to express your disappointment and then move on to the next thing in your life. You continue to have hope that good things are happening for you and, in the end, good things do happen for you because you continue trying again until you find what you were looking for.

In either direction, ditching your absolutes and staying open and curious is the way to go.

CHAPTER 15

COME AT ME, BRO

LISTEN HERE, tough guy—in some situations, your resilience, mental toughness, and stubbornness are going to be your saving grace. That's right: the same stubbornness that has had you refusing to express your emotions or to try new things because of your anxiety is the same stubbornness that you can use to actually help you overcome your anxiety—if you direct it the right way.

Building your mental toughness can help you handle new things and take unwanted outcomes or situations with ease and grace, if you are willing to stay committed to your strength. When you are mentally tough, staying open and staying dedicated to the outcome you want even if the path does not look clear-cut is a lot easier. This way, you are not as likely to respond with anxiety or extreme fear or discomfort any and every time something does not go the way you planned it. Instead, you find yourself with the ability to simply and painlessly maneuver onto a different path when the present one is not working out for you.

You allow yourself to feel confident and empowered when you are growing, which means that you are able to keep growing, even when it looks like your growth is not going to be as easy as you expected it would be. I mean, come on, is achieving growth ever actually easy? Even a tree has to start as a seed that has to totally crack open and shatter in the dirt before it starts to grow, and then it has to remain buried and be completely enveloped in dirt and darkness with no end in sight before it even turns into something big enough to barely peek above the soil. And we're still not even close to being a full grown tree yet.

Are you willing to remain buried and be completely enveloped in dirt and darkness with no end in sight before you see an iota of progress? Let's be honest, no growth is going to be easy or effortless. Everything you desire to do that has any significant outcome in life is almost always going to bring about pain and discomfort. You can't just cower into a freak-out episode every time the going gets a little tough. Feeling strong enough to look your challenges in the face and say "Come at me, bro" is the beginning of feeling confident and capable, and forcing your anxiety to start to dwindle.

But when you lack mental toughness, to put it simply, your mind does not work for you. Instead of helping you feel confident and comfortable with navigating new situations, your mind will make you feel incapable and completely freaked out every time something new comes your way.

Rather than adapting with change and riding the waves of life, you'll be more like the inexperienced surfer who gets sucked under by a wave every time, and trapped in seaweed, struggling to get yourself back to the surface.

A lack of mental toughness can be frustrating, especially when you can see how things could be better, yet you cannot figure out how to actually do better. Many people who lack mental toughness beat themselves up over their mental weakness every time they find that their own thinking patterns and behaviors prevent them from achieving the life that they desire. This self-deprecating behavior can lead to even more mental weakness, making it even harder for you to effectively get through anything that life faces you with.

If you do not get a grip on your brain and start taking things on with confidence and strength—you can pretty much guarantee that you are going to always live with anxiety. You will always bounce around in life, always being pushed around by circumstance. The more that you're pushed around, the lower you will feel, and the worse it will all get. As a result, you will find yourself being completely destroyed by everyone and everything around you until eventually, you wonder if you can even take it anymore. Oftentimes, people who are living in this deep state of mental weakness feel like they are going to go bonkers at any given moment because they feel so frustrated that it seems like no matter what, they just can't handle anything. Fortunately, it is possible to give yourself control over your mind and experiences and move forward with confidence and intention.

And as a matter of fact, I happen to have written an entire book about it called *Make Your Brain Your Bitch.* Yes, it's currently available on Amazon and Audible. Yes, you will love it and you should get it. And yes, we'll get back to the rest of this book now.

Work Those Mental Muscles

You may or may not be surprised that learning to increase your mental toughness or mental endurance happens in a way that is largely similar to increasing your physical endurance. When you want to increase your physical endurance, you get in the gym and pump iron like a maniac for eighteen hours straight until your muscles are ripped and you are perfect. It happens overnight. Right? *Wrong!* Increasing your physical endurance comes from taking your time, repeating the same mundane practices over and over, and gradually increasing the intensity until you reach your goal.

The same thing goes for building your mental endurance: you need to continue practicing mental toughness building strategies on a small level until your mind is strong enough to handle everything that is being thrown your way. Now, it is important to understand that by this we do not mean that nothing is going to phase you. You are not Chuck Norris. You are not going to be able to just look at life in the face and take absolutely everything that comes your way without ever breaking down.

People with mental toughness still feel fear, confusion, anger, disappointment, sadness, frustration, and pain. They simply know that even though they are experiencing these emotions, they will be able to get through them and come out on the other side okay, and satisfied with how they handled themselves along the way. If they are not satisfied, they will review why they are not satisfied, and then they will put in the work toward changing their behaviors so that they can handle themselves better in the future.

A great way to practice building up your mental toughness muscles is to stay in the shit. Whenever something gets hard and you feel the urge to flee, stay anyway. Now, I don't mean if you come across a grizzly bear, stay anyway. I'm talking the little things, the non-life threatening things...the ones that anxiety causes to feel like they are big, life threatening things. For example, if you start to get uncomfortable in a conversation because everyone's voiced their opinion on the latest presidential election and now it's your turn and you have a different opinion, don't flee, don't change the subject. Stay in it and voice your opinion.

Over time, you will start to take the power from all of these circumstances that used to induce anxiety in you and you'll have the strength to sit through tougher and tougher situations with perfect ease and calm.

Increase Your Trust In Yourself

Another way that you can begin increasing your mental endurance is by having more trust in yourself. If you are constantly going through life thinking that you are going to dagger yourself in the back as a result of your unreliable actions, chances are, you are going to struggle to grow your mental endurance and release your anxiety.

You need to build more trust in yourself so that you can overcome the false belief that you are not trustworthy enough to have your own back. As you do this, your mental endurance will increase because you will no longer need to put so much effort into making sure that you are going to be okay in all situations: you will trust that you have what it takes to keep yourself okay in all situations.

Instead of getting the shakes before going into a job interview, you will feel confident enough to be able to trust yourself to make a positive impression. Your trust in yourself develops confidence in yourself, which enables you to live a better life in general, with significantly fewer run-ins with our old friend anxiety.

How do you do this? Simple. Trusting yourself comes from making promises to yourself and keeping them, taking care of yourself, and honoring your needs whenever they arise. The more you show yourself that you can be trusted with looking out for your best interest, the more trust you are going to have in yourself, which means you will be more capable of releasing your anxiety. Your fear of having things go terribly wrong and being unable to take care of them if they do will be minimized as you begin to understand that everything will work out just fine because at the end of the day, you can handle it, and you've got your back.

CHAPTER 16

CUT THE CRAP

IF YOUR CAR'S center console is filled with gum wrappers and balled up napkins, your wallet is stuffed with faded receipts dated before Britney Spears' *Hit Me Baby One More Time* tour, and the inside of your house looks like it could be eligible for its own TLC show (the kind that people watch to feel better about themselves), you need to start looking at your environment as a potential source of your anxiety. Our physical environments have been proven to contribute to anxiety when we have too much clutter in our surroundings.

A 2009 study conducted at UCLA came to an interesting conclusion. While doing home tours, it was discovered that women who would characterize their home environments as "cluttered" had saliva samples that revealed that they had higher levels of cortisol (a hormone secreted in times of stress) than women who would not characterize their homes as being cluttered.

But even without that study, I'm sure we all know from firsthand experience how much more difficult everything is and how much worse everything feels when your space is a mess. Clutter translates to visual noise, which can seem very "loud" to your eyes if you have clutter everywhere. This is why some people instantly feel overwhelmed in a certain place. And this is why you find it harder to think straight, think clearly, or think at all when your place is in disarray. Your eyes have so much new information to take in, and so do all of your other senses.

And the negative effect of clutter doesn't stop there. A 2016 study at Cornell University took a group of just over 100 students and placed some in your standard, neat, run-of-the-mill, clean kitchen, and placed the remainder in a cluttered, messy kitchen. Then, they gave them cookies. The students in the more chaotic kitchens ate more cookies than the students in the uncluttered kitchen, indicating that environmental clutter can make you vulnerable to a poor mindset that causes you to make worse decisions. And think about it—the negative consequences of those decisions can of course lead to anxiety.

So it does not matter whether you use the KonMari method of tidying up, the 20/10 method, or the throw-everything-into-a-giant-pile-and-light-it-on-fire method: as long as you can cut the crap from your life, you are going to start feeling a lot better. You can start with your physical surroundings, but you should also move on to your mental surroundings, too. After all, keeping a cluttered environment can lead to having a cluttered mind, which can contribute to keeping a cluttered environment, thus creating a wild spiral of clutter in your entire life that ends with you sobbing on an episode of *Hoarders* wondering how things got this far.

If you don't want that to be you, I recommend you check out my other book on cutting the crap, also available on Amazon and Audible. I know, I know, I just plugged another book—sorry, what can I say, I write a lot of books! Anywho, let's just go over some tips right here and right now to help you cut the crap from your life.

Eliminate Clutter From Your Space

The first thing you want to do is start eliminating clutter from your physical space. In general, there are three physical spaces in our lives where we keep clutter: our homes, our cars, and our work environments. If you can't see the floor in your house, you can't see the dashboard in your car, and you can't see the desk in your office, these are signs that you may have a clutter problem.

When we have a lot of physical clutter around us that looks junky and even gross, we often begin to feel embarrassed and ashamed, which can lead to poor or fewer social engagements and put a damper on our personal relationships. Who wants to invite someone over to their place when it looks like the *Hoarders* filming crew just left it? This can spiral and create intense anxiety fast, so learning how to keep your space clutter-free and clean will not only help you feel less stressed by having a cleaner space, but also by no longer having to cower in shame every time someone comes over and sees your gross house. In addition to helping alleviate feelings of guilt and shame, having a clean space will also help you actually find what you are looking for, which is helpful, too. Who's ever gone into a full-blown anxiety attack when you couldn't find your keys and you were already running late to something important? You can't see me, but I'm raising my hand over here. And I can't see you, but I'm willing to bet you're raising your hand over there as well.

The best way to clean your physical space is to start by taking out the trash. Start with the obvious trash (the gum wrappers, fast food containers, and such). Then move on to the things you think you need for "someday maybe," "just in case," or "sentimental value" that you actually have never looked at, used, or thought about for the past six years—yeah, that's actually trash too. Then, make your way to the hidden trash (yes, I'm talking about your junk drawer and that hidden corner of your closet you forbid anyone to see). Just because you can't see it, doesn't mean it's not there. When there's too much garbage in your space, it tends to get mixed into the belongings you actually need and care about, which can create a horrible mess, and make it hard for you to see or find what you're looking for.

Eliminating garbage often eliminates a big portion of the mess that you have surrounded yourself with. Once the garbage is gone, start organizing the remains based on what you want to give away, what you want to sell, and what you want to keep. Then, for what's left to keep, clean it if it's dirty, then organize it in a way that makes it easy for you to find but doesn't contribute to visual clutter.

Finally, you want to make sure that when you are done decluttering everything, you actually maintain that decluttered state. Nothing is more frustrating than having your space finally cleaned up, only to have it get all messy again, as this will only create feelings of defeat and failure. Maintaining your clean space keeps you organized and feeling less anxious in general, so it may be important to listen to your mom and keep your room clean and your bed made. Fortunately, once you have decluttered, keeping your space, your life, and your mind clutter-free is actually not too hard, as long as you stay committed and continue putting in the work daily.

For your physical space, get into the habit of putting things in their rightful place right away, immediately after you are done using them. This way, you do not have to put anything away later, or do some big cleanup day later because you have already kept everything organized throughout the day. In addition to this, you should also set aside a few minutes every day to get a little cleaning done so you don't have to go into a panic and run around like a chicken with no head every single time someone wants to come to your house and hang out with you. Another reason why cleaning up on a daily basis is important is because—let's be honest—when you plan a big spring cleaning day, you do *not* clean up on the day that you said you were going to. If you did, your brain would not be fried from the stress of living like you are packed in a sardine can.

Lastly, give up pointless shopping and spending. Not only is it fiscally irresponsible to unnecessarily spend more money than you need to, but it also creates worry by giving you way too much stuff to have to keep clean and organized in your house, and it just contributes to the clutter. The less you have in your house, the less money you are spending, *and* the less you have to clean. Those minimalists are definitely on to something.

Eliminate Clutter From Your Life

In addition to eliminating clutter from your environment, you also want to eliminate clutter from your life. Eliminating clutter from your life means releasing any person, place, or thing that does not genuinely contribute to your happiness, mental peace, or ensuring you have positive life experiences. For example, say you are feeling anxious, and you look into your lifestyle and realize that you spend a lot of time at crowded hangouts that have tacky decorations on every inch of every wall, and it's always overrun with people yelling over each other just so they can hear their own conversations. This might be a place you eliminate from your life. There's a reason why kids are always ten times more excited to go to Six Flags than parents are. While certain places can definitely be fun, spending most of your life in crowded, visually stressful environments can be overwhelming and...well, stressful. Eliminating these environments from your life, or at least not going as frequently, can be a great way to minimize the stress that you are feeling from the multitude of things happening in your physical space.

Decluttering your relationships can be helpful, too, especially if you find that you have been surrounding yourself with people that you do not necessarily resonate with in your life. It can be easy to want to stay around people who are comfortable and familiar to you, but all too often, we surround ourselves with people who feel familiar and comfortable for those reasons alone. If you are not actually feeling like these are positive relationships to be engaging in any longer, the people that you've outgrown, or just plain don't like anymore, may be bringing you more stress than benefits.

Having known someone since the beginning of time is not a good enough reason to justify maintaining that relationship if the relationship is somehow toxic, draining, or no longer serves you. You may feel that adjusting or eliminating the relationship could be too overwhelming, making it not worth the mental anxiety from having to have the difficult "break up" conversation. But trust me, holding on to low quality relationships is even more painful long term. So rip off the band-aid in the interest of releasing misaligned friendships, which will not only result in eliminating anxiety, but steering you forward towards personal growth in your life in general.

Finally, focus on decluttering your schedule. Listen, if

your schedule looks like a total nightmare, if you are doing things every two minutes, and if you never have a break, you are going to be anxious, no doubt about it. You can't cram your schedule full of tasks and then find yourself running late to all of them because you are stretched too thin, and then wonder why on earth your nerves are frayed and your world is always spinning around you.

The reality is: your time management skills suck and you need to get yourself together! Organize your schedule better, give yourself plenty of time between appointments and commitments, and light a fire under your ass so that you actually get moving. Don't overwhelm yourself with too many commitments, and don't procrastinate and lollygag to the commitments you do choose to keep. If you are not respecting your own time and are driving yourself up the wall with too many commitments or with an inability to get yourself together and show up on time, your poor time management skills are seriously screwing you and also having a negative effect on the people around you.

Having too much on your plate is not only overwhelming, but it's also ineffective. Having every minute of every day full is just leading to you having higher stress and lower performance long term. Do you want to have to redo everything because you were so stressed out that you didn't do it right the first time? Do you want your life to whizz by you while you're a complete zombie who can't even remember what they had for breakfast this morning? Do you want to be too mentally exhausted to even be able to show up properly in your relationships? I'm going to assume you answered no on all questions. Everything you do with your time should feel enjoyable or like it serves you in some way so you are not feeling the stress, regret, guilt, and anxiety that come from never having a moment to breathe or doing too many things you don't really want to do.

So to avoid having to be *that* person, you can instead give your schedule a makeover and start focusing on creating one that is more realistic and manageable for you. Strive to always have at least 2 hours a day to do nothing. If that's not enough for you to not be eternally stressed and you still feel like you always have to be somewhere at all times, then add even more buffer. As a result of having a lot more time for relaxation, you will find yourself feeling a lot less stressed out, and generally feeling more at peace in your life. The time off in your life actually makes you more effective for the time "on."

Eliminate Clutter From Your Mind

Your mind is another place where clutter can really pile up. Oftentimes, if your life is cluttered, so is your mind, whether you realize it or not, which is why you see physical clutter in your space, too. Your mind typically carries the clutter of unexpressed emotions, painful memories, to-do lists, task sheets, movie quotes, obnoxious song lyrics, and many other different random pieces of data that float around in your brain and refuse to make their way out. Part of this is having poor mindset behaviors and habits that allow unnecessary data to remain hardwired into your brain, and the other part of this is having poor management skills when it comes to dealing with the clutter in your brain in the first place. So, if your brain is cluttered, this means you probably suck at both preventing clutter from getting there in the first place and managing clutter once it naturally arises.

Fortunately, this is something that you can easily fix with a few lifestyle changes that prompt you to take a closer look at how you are currently using your mind, and how you can use it better to keep mental clutter from creating chaos. One thing you can do is start taking note of what thoughts you are having on a regular basis throughout the day so that you can start getting an idea of what is causing your mind to feel chaotic in the first place. The pain diary that you will learn about in Chapter 22 is a great opportunity for you to get clear on what you are feeding your brain and how you are feeling about that content. Another great idea is to wear a bracelet or a band on one arm and then switch it to your other arm any time you notice that you are holding on to thoughts that are contributing to you feeling anxious or chaotic. This is actually a subliminal programming strategy that allows you to draw awareness to your mental patterns and break state so that you are not staying consumed in strategies that do not effectively serve your growth.

Next, you can start paying attention to how you are managing important information as it comes in. For example, if you are scheduling a new appointment with your doctor, rather than pretending that you will remember it, writing it down on your arm with a pen, or writing it down on the back of a balled up old receipt, have a permanent place to keep track of appointments like this. Using a calendar app in your phone or on a planner that you keep on you at all times is a great way to ensure that every appointment you schedule is accounted for and that you never forget what you are supposed to be doing or where you are supposed to be. You can do this with any information, too, not just new appointments.

Richard Branson, multi-billionaire owner of The Virgin Group, swears by carrying a notebook around and having a note open in his phone where he writes down information all day long. This is how he keeps track of appointments, any information he finds interesting, ideas he has, and things he wants to do or see—and then at the end of the day, he organizes all of the information as needed. This way, he never forgets anything, whether he needs to remember to pick up the toilet paper or visit the grand opening of a brand new Virgin gym. And most importantly, his mind gets to stay clear so it can be used for what the brain is best used for: processing information and making decisions, not storing information. If it works for a billionaire, surely, it can work for you.

LIKE WHAT YOU SEE SO FAR?

BRAGGING ON THE INTERNET CAN SOMETIMES BE A
GOOD THING.

THIS IS ONE OF THOSE TIMES.

LEAVE A REVIEW ON AMAZON, BRAGGING ABOUT HOW
AWESOME YOU ARE FOR READING THIS BOOK.

CHAPTER 17

DROP THE CUP OF POISON

LIKE IT OR NOT, you may be a big part of the reason that you are anxious. If you have a cup of poison, you know it's poison, yet you are constantly pulling that cup up to your lips and taking swig after swig by way of allowing yourself to continue every single bad habit and behavior that makes you anxious, then you only have yourself to blame. You can't continually drink poison and expect to not die a slow and miserable death. The more you continue to engage in unhealthy and self-sabotaging behaviors, the more your anxiety is going to grow, and the less trusting of yourself you are going to become. Put the cup of poison down.

If you have been filling your life with anxiety with either bad habits or ineffective band-aid solutions, it is time to look yourself in the mirror and give your head a shake. Instead of admitting defeat or believing something is wrong with you, we're going to find areas where you can take responsibility for all the chaos that you are experiencing. If you are suffering from a mental condition or deep psychological trauma, seek professional help, as attempting to override certain behaviors on your own may not be ideal or even possible if you are truly struggling on a more severe than average level.

But if you are just a regular Joe or Jane who knocks back a half a bottle of wine to "loosen up" before a date, dodges people because you want to avoid confrontation, or keeps your lips sealed in work meetings because you're afraid of saying something stupid, stop it. There are some simple behavior alterations very easily within your control that can be used to ease your behavioral responses to anxiety. If you want to chill out, bro, you need to take a look at your current actions and start picking new ones. If you don't, you're going to find yourself constantly at the mercy of your own heinous behaviors, wondering why you're not doing better or feeling better about life when, in reality, you are your own worst enemy.

I mean think about it, if you are constantly drinking when you are sad, or smoking weed when you are stressed, or sleeping through hangouts because you don't want to admit to your friend Becky that you do not care about her dog's half birthday party, how do you think you are going to acquire the life skills to handle...life? Instead of fixing the root of your problems, you are literally bending your behavior to fit around poor coping methods because you are unwilling to face your issues and generate real, healthy coping methods that are actually going to, you know, *help you.*

Identify Where You're Sipping The Poison

Releasing your unhealthy habits and behaviors starts with first identifying what exactly you are doing in response to situations that make you feel anxious. Then, take a step further—or really, a step back—and identify why the heck you feel the need to engage in these behaviors in the first place. Is it because you always have and you feel like you are not allowed to change? Is it because you have developed a group of friends who also engage in this behavior and you're afraid of how they'll respond to you if you stop? Is it because you believe that doing something, or not doing something, will make you a bad person? Is it because you are afraid to admit something about yourself to yourself, so it's easier to just cover it up and ignore it instead of going to a painful place within you?

Get really clear on why you are engaging in these unwanted behaviors in the first place. The more awareness you have around yourself and your overwhelming unconscious need to engage in these ultimately unhealthy habitual actions, the more you are going to be able to recognize when they are happening and then replace them with healthier behaviors that reach the same goal of making that anxious feeling go away.

If you have many unhealthy anxiety coping behaviors, avoid trying to adjust every single one at once because you are only going to make yourself more anxious. Instead, focus on one or two of the biggest culprits first, and once you've overcome them, slowly snowball from there to ensure that you are not trying to change your entire persona in one go. Rome wasn't built in a day, ya know. Attempting to rewrite too much of your reality at a single time can be overwhelming and ineffective, so be realistic about what you can achieve.

Find New Coping Strategies

After you have identified how and why you're screwing yourself, it's time to unscrew yourself. Unscrewing yourself starts with learning where your coping methods are failing so that you can start finding new opportunities for them to go right. Get clear on why your present coping methods are failing and what it is that you are trying to achieve with these methods so that you have a big picture understanding of what your real goal is.

For example, if you drink wine when you are stressed and it never ends well, ask yourself what it is about drinking wine that helps you feel like you are no longer stressed and what you are really trying to achieve with that wine. Are you trying to slow down your heart rate, so you feel physically more relaxed? Instead of drinking wine, you could meditate or do yoga to achieve the same result. Are you trying to take your mind off of the thing that's causing you the stress? Instead of drinking, you could call a friend, doodle, clean your closet...there are a number of activities that could be used to replace drinking. When you know what your actual goal is with your coping method, you can easily find a strategy that is healthier, but just as effective in reducing your stress and anxiety.

So start getting clear on all of your coping methods. Dig 'em all up—good, bad, and ugly. And evaluate and reevaluate them one by one. Identify which ones are healthy and can stay the same, and which ones are unhealthy and need to change. Oftentimes, when you are undergoing a revealing healing process like this, as you begin uncovering and fixing some coping methods, you will discover that there are even more that you hadn't noticed previously. This is a great chance for you to ~~start noticing how really screwed up you are~~ get a grip and realize how many opportunities you have to heal yourself and improve your life. If you are already in the process of revising and improving several coping methods, as others come to mind that you would like to bring your awareness to and work on in the future, simply write them down. You'll get to them later.

As you are making your way through the list of all the dysfunctional habits that you need to work towards eliminating, you should also make a note to give yourself time. Looking at your list, realize how long ago you developed these dysfunctional habits and how long it took you to reinforce them, so that you can be more realistic as to how long it is actually going to take for you to replace them. After all, if you've been doing the same thing for ten years, it is unlikely for you to change it overnight. Lasting change comes from repeatedly making new decisions.

Now, this does not mean that you should be lazy and use the fact that it will take time to make these transitions as a reason to procrastinate and avoid doing the actual work itself. Instead, it means that you should focus on getting your shit together and working steadily and consistently toward your resolve while also being patient with yourself if your shifts do not happen as quickly as you hoped they would.

Replace Your Old Behaviors With New Ones

Once you have identified what new habits you want to replace your old habits with, it is time for you to start doing the real work on making shifts in your life. This part is easier for you to achieve if you understand what is happening in your brain each time something signals anxious feelings within you, so let's take a moment to look at the psychology behind what's triggering your anxiety, and why it's impacting you the way that it is.

Each time you have a little anxiety-trigger pulled, say someone says something snide to you and you feel upset with them, your brain has been trained to respond in a certain way. Perhaps as soon as something unkind is said to you, you instantly feel inferior, and you begin to try to make that person like you because you feel intensely hurt inside by the fact that they seem to be disinterested in you or they are disapproving of you in some way. Maybe you abandon your own values and beliefs about life in order to start people-pleasing because you feel a deep sense of hurt when people do not like you.

As a result, you begin to feel anxiety because you are not only hurting that this person does not like you, but you are also hurting by your response, which seems to also indicate to you that you do not fully like yourself, either. This automatic response that leads to feelings of inadequacy, unworthiness, self-deprecation, and anxiety could be shifted to have you instead respond in a way that has you affirm your value to yourself. You may begin to validate yourself through your own words and actions, and accept and release the fact that another person does not like you, or that they do not like something that you did or said.

When you are in the process of replacing behaviors, it is important to understand that the way you have been responding for years is hardwired into your brain through your neural pathways, which is why this has become an automatic response. For that reason, you should understand that each time you consciously choose to behave in a new way, you are forming new neural pathways and weakening your old ones.

At first, your old, unwanted neural pathway is going to be a stubborn son of a bitch. It is not going anywhere without a fight. Your old neural pathways are going to be extremely strong, and your new ones are going to be weak and unfamiliar, which is why it is going to feel like it takes you so long to get over your shit already. Over time, however, as you continue to choose new strategies consciously, your old subconscious ones will be erased, and you will be able to more easily and effortlessly respond with your new and improved conscious responses. Repetition and time are key here. You don't change a habit by doing something once and only once. You change a habit by doing something over and over and over again...even when it's hard and you don't want to and it feels so much easier and more comfortable to just go back to your old ways.

Rewiring your brain can be challenging, but with consistent, strategic, conscious changes, you will make yourself proud of the way that you are growing as a person, your brain will be feeling brand spanking new, and you'll find that the things that used to put you over the edge no longer have that level of power over you that they used to.

Be Willing To Let It Go

When you are in the process of recovering from anxiety, it can be easy to deny that the behaviors you are engaging in are actually producing anxiety in your life. As you're going through your coping strategies and determining which should stay, and which should go, be as objective and ruthless as possible. Many people want to justify their anxiety-inducing coping strategies as being fine because they don't want to let go of them. Yes, in the short-term, those four shots of espresso make you feel like you can conquer meetings at work. Sure, those three glasses of wine make a trip to your in-laws' a lot easier. But remember, these strategies (and many like them) are band-aid solutions that ultimately lead to higher anxiety in the future.

The more you ignore the development and the root causes of your anxiety and engage in these quickie so-called "solutions," the more you are going to feel like you are unable to cope in the long run. Eventually, even your current unhealthy coping strategies will become useless as your anxiety grows so large that it cannot be contained by these band-aids any longer. So what's the solution? No, you don't need a bigger band-aid. No, you don't need four glasses of wine instead of three. You need to be honest and admit to yourself the behaviors that you are engaging in that are ultimately causing yourself and your anxiety more harm than good. Here, detachment is important as you learn to detach from the idea that these are effective coping methods and instead choose to become more open-minded towards a potentially better alternative.

Since I still don't trust you, and just somehow get the feeling that you're mentally white-knuckling some of your bad habits, I'll make it plain and give you a list of some of these common problems disguised as solutions. Some of the most common issues that people deny having any adverse effect on their anxiety include things like drinking caffeine, drinking alcohol, using drugs (including marijuana—I don't care if it's legal or that it's a "natural herb"), smoking (the classic or new fancy way), poor quality diet, extreme exercise habits, to name a few.

If smoking a joint makes you paranoid, caffeine makes you jittery, and alcohol makes you drunk and make stupid decisions, those things are doing more harm than good to you. If something makes you feel better in one way, but worse in another, that's no bueno. So be honest with yourself and figure out what you need to moderate, what you need to manage, and what you need to eliminate and replace altogether.

CHAPTER 18

WHEN IN DOUBT, DO WEIRD THINGS THAT WEIRD PEOPLE DO

NOW, you know that I am a fan of logic and practicality, and generally prefer to steer clear of the hippy dippy, flowers-in-your-hair, granola-in-your-pocket type stuff, but I would be doing you a disservice if I didn't at least mention a few practices that have actually proven to be beneficial to some people. So, I just consolidated them all into one brief chapter. You're welcome.

The fact is, things like meditation, mindfulness, yoga, and sensual raisin eating (yes, you heard that right) have all brought great relief to many people struggling with anxiety. For you, understanding these methods and incorporating them on top of logical or science-based methods may be the perfect pairing to help you relieve yourself of your own anxiety.

Meditation

Here's one you've probably never heard of before.

Kidding. Meditation has been proven to slow down your heart rate and reduce your racing thoughts—if you are doing it correctly. Harvard neuroscientist Sara Lazar found that it also has the potential to reduce the density of the amygdala, a portion of the brain that plays a key role in helping us process anxiety, stress, and fear—the theory being that the reduced stress prompts the brain to alter itself accordingly, needing only to manage a lighter psychological load.

When done properly, meditation is meant to help you by having you physically relax your body, which can lead to you having an easier time relaxing your mind, as well. When you take the time to stop and meditate, you give yourself the space you need to breathe deeply, calm your body, and calm your mind. For some people, sitting around and deep breathing is all they need to feel more at ease in their lives. If your problem is that you do not have enough quiet time in your life to sit and breathe deeply because you're constantly flitting from one thing to the next like a bumblebee with ADHD, sounds like you're the person that needs this the most to reduce their anxiety.

Of course, it is important that you learn how to properly meditate, as nothing will drive your anxiety up higher than sitting in your quietness and allowing your mind to continue racing and your body to continue freaking out. If you are sitting in meditation while tense, fidgeting, and thinking about how horrible you are at this because you are horrible at everything in life, and you use this as a time to sink even deeper into your anxious spiral, then naturally, meditation is not going to help you.

Mindfulness

Mindfulness is often a part of meditation, but it can also be practiced on its own. When you are practicing mindfulness, your goal is to stop getting overwhelmed by your thoughts and to start engaging deeper into your present reality so that you can feel more "grounded" and "centered." On a psychological level, what mindfulness is actually doing is teaching you that you are safer than you think and that you are not actually about to get eaten by a ravenous pack of dogs or a dangerous, big kitty jungle cat. You are simply overreacting, and you need to bring yourself back into the moment and realize that in this moment, you are fine.

You are a modern human with modern human problems that typically do not involve spontaneous death by being hunted down by something hungry. In the olden days, an overwhelmed and anxious response was natural to small threats, but these days, your intensely anxious response to your stapler running out of staples during a meeting that no one is paying attention to anyway, is truly not necessary. You can easily go refill the stapler and carry on, and chances are, no one at your office is going to eat you along the way. Except maybe Bill. He was always a weird one. You've got to watch out for Bill.

Mindfulness can often start with using your senses to bring you back into reality. Here's a five-step method that the "gurus" like to use:

You start by seeing five different things and giving them basic mental descriptions in your head. For example, "white book page with a redundant description of mindfulness practice.

Then, you move on to four different things that you can touch. For example, "smooth book cover of hilarious, yet helpful book for coping with anxiety."

Next, you move on to three things that you can hear, for example, "annoying neighbor who has been cutting their lawn for three hours straight." How big is their lawn, anyway?

After that, you want to think about two things that you can smell. Now, unless you are comfortable with sticking your nose in a plant in a public place and inhaling deeply like this is your first day on earth, you may benefit from keeping a couple of scented things on you for these practices. A tube of ChapStick and some cologne or perfume on your arm before you leave the house are two great scented tools that you can call on any time the need strikes to practice mindfulness with the help of your sense of smell.

Lastly, you want to think of one thing that you can taste. Unless you can burp on command to catch a late afternoon rerun of your breakfast burrito, you can carry something with you at all times like gum or small candies that you can snack on when you need to ground.

Yoga

Yoga, though it often entails physical contortion of the body, is helpful for un-contorting the brain. Focusing on the movement of your body is helpful for the mind because it can get you out of your head. Science says that any exercise is beneficial, as it allows you to use up the adrenaline in your body and bring calmness back to within, but the "gurus" swear that it has to be yoga. The physical aspect of yoga usually involves slow stretching that allows you to completely work out every muscle in your body—if you're doing it properly. If you're not doing it properly, you probably fell asleep in child's pose and won't wake up until everyone else has left the room...after pointing and laughing at you, of course.

There are different types of yoga that have different focuses...foci...focuses? Ah, whatever. Here's what I suggest. Try a form of yoga that requires you to move your muscles as much as possible. Vinyasa Flow is a perfect method for that. Don't judge me for knowing that. I swear, I don't have flowers in my hair. The stretching helps release your adrenaline and move it through your body so that you are no longer holding on to it and letting it fester. With anxiety, holding on to the energy can quickly turn into you becoming irritable and angry because your anxiety was not allowed to effectively work its way out, meaning that you are instead bottling it up. An ever-filling bottle that is never emptied is bound to explode. So, instead of holding that anxious energy in, you can release it through yoga and let yourself be at peace again. Or, you know, you could join a spin class, go kickboxing, running, swimming, skateboarding, unicycling, parkour, or do any other number of physical activities that will also use up your adrenaline.

Dietary Adjustments

Your diet can contribute to your anxiety in a big way—let's not deny that. In fact, we have already discussed how alcohol and caffeine intake can increase your anxiety and leave you at greater risk for an episode. However, there are said to be other ways that your diet can impact your anxiety as well—one way being how your existing diet can increase your anxiety, and the other being how you can modify your diet to actually decrease your anxiety.

According to...science, people may experience an increase in anxiety if they are consuming things that they have an allergy or intolerance toward because it can increase the amount of stress being put on your body. This may seem obvious, but many of us are actually suffering from allergies we're not even aware of, so we're wondering why we're feeling so bad, meanwhile, we're just mindlessly shoveling in the very thing that's causing the problem.

So going out and getting an official allergy test might be a good early birthday present to yourself. The more you eat something that is not good for you, the harder of a time your body has to fight to undo the damage that you are doing. The same can go for junk foods or foods that are universally not good for you, as your body has to work harder to process them and gain nutrition from them while preventing them from doing damage on your body.

The other way that you can use your diet to manage your anxiety is by eating things that are known to decrease anxiety. Herbs like chamomile and lavender are known for their physical relaxation powers, so eating foods or drinking teas with these herbs added in them can support you in reducing your anxious responses. Brazil nuts, fatty fish, eggs, pumpkin seeds, dark chocolate, turmeric, and yogurt are also said to be helpful in this regard due to how they work with the body as suppressants rather than stimulants.

Aromatherapy

Aromatherapy is said to help people deal with anxiety in an effective way, and this particular strategy, "woo woo" as it may sound, actually has a scientific explanation. Aromatherapy works through the olfactory system which allows essential oils and other scented products to pass through the blood-brain barrier and affect the body just like consuming actual herbs would do. Another way that the olfactory system works is by triggering the limbic system, which essentially means that when you inhale something, it can remind you of positive memories which can bring peace back into your mind. If when you were a kid, you had fun growing up near a lake that had many wildflowers growing around it, any time you smell wildflowers, you might find yourself inadvertently going back to your happy place. So the trigger of the positive memory could perk up your mood and immediately make you feel happy.

So, with aromatherapy, you can choose to inhale something that's a general "smell good" favorite, like essential oils of lavender, chamomile, or lemon balm—or you can get a little more custom with it and inhale something that triggers a positive memory. When it comes to using herbs, essential oils especially, it is important that you use them in a safe way, as there actually is a such thing as too much of a good thing. Despite what many self-proclaimed aromatherapists or MLM peddlers might tell you, there are precautions that need to be taken to avoid damaging yourself with essential oils. A few such precautions are to never put essential oils directly on your skin without diluting first, never diffuse too much at once, and exercise caution when diffusing around animals or children. So make sure that if you choose this route, you do your due diligence and get guidance from a credible source. No, I'm not talking about that weird guy in hemp pants who's always circling your block, selling unmarked bottles of liquid for fifty cents apiece.

P.S. We have reached the end of the chapter. If you are disappointed that we have reached the end of the chapter without going in depth on sensual raisin eating, I apologize and ask for your forgiveness. But Google can help pick up the slack here.

PART 4

THE BIG GUNS

CHAPTER 19

REWIRE YOUR BRAIN

SOUNDS EASY ENOUGH, right? Just like a computer. It doesn't do anything it's not programmed to do. And if you want it to do something different, you have to re-program it. Mental health professionals are big fans of teaching their patients how to rewire their brains to help them experience healthier mental processes. The way they do this is by helping people understand the cycles of their brain so they can begin to break these cycles intentionally. One very effective tool for this is known as Cognitive Behavioral Therapy (CBT), a form of therapy that simply helps people identify unhealthy cycles and replace them with new ones.

How CBT Works

If you are digging into CBT, you are really pulling out the big guns, as you are calling on a therapy-based approach to your anxiety. The benefit of using CBT is just that—it is used in therapy, so the strategies are systematic and very thought out, meaning that you are more likely to gain relief from utilizing it. CBT was identified by Aaron T. Beck back in the 1950s when he was studying depression and how it impacts the brain, and he discovered that people with depression were having abnormal, automatic thoughts that were triggering the onset of depression. Following this discovery, it was realized that the same thing was taking place in the brain when people had unusual or abnormal experiences with anxiety.

Using CBT to help cure anxiety is a practice that begins with identifying what your automatic thoughts are that are causing your anxiety in the first place. Automatic thoughts are essentially thoughts that we think automatically in response to a certain trigger. For example, if you see a pig flying, you might automatically be triggered to remember that time when your weird aunt said she would quit smoking when pigs fly. Also, if you see a pig flying, you might have bigger problems than anxiety, but anywho...

If you are anxious, your automatic thoughts that are being triggered are what's causing you to have intense flashes of anxiety. Once you have identified your automatic thoughts, you will discover all of the behaviors, feelings, and outcomes that go with these thoughts so that you can get a full understanding of how they are impacting you. Then, you can go on to choose a new way that you wish to respond to your automatic thoughts so that you do not have the same responses. Often, your shifted response will also come alongside the practice of you consciously choosing to see through your automatic thoughts and choosing new thoughts that you can begin teaching yourself to think instead. This way, your new automatic thoughts stimulate neutrality or something positive, rather than intense anxiety.

Plot Out Your Cycle

In order to start using CBT in your healing, you need to begin with plotting out your cycle. You can do this by considering a time where you typically experience anxiety and then taking the time to recognize what the cycle around that trigger is. You may discover that your cycle is relatively small and straight forward, or you may discover that it is complex and that it takes you some time to fully understand where all elements of the cycle are coming from. Either way, the more you stop to reflect on your cycle, the more information you are going to have, so it's best not to rush this part of the process.

Typically, the cycles that coincide with your anxiety start with you observing something (a trigger), then have you go on to interpret that thing, which becomes a thought, which then turns into your emotional response of anxiety. For example, maybe when you were five years old, you saw a mascot of a big yellow monkey, and it terrified you because you perceived it as a threat, and you thought you were in danger, so you became anxious. Now, any time you see mascots or monkeys, you find yourself automatically thinking that you are in danger because of that childhood experience.

If you want to use CBT, you need to identify the anxiety, the thought, and the reason why you are having that thought. You can also take the time to identify what other mental and physical symptoms you were having when the cycle was going on, as the more information you have about it, the more prepared you can be when it comes to dealing with it. For example, maybe in your mind, you began to have repeating thoughts, and your palms grew sweaty, and your back stiffened up, which lead to you recognizing that you were feeling anxious.

When you plot out the cycle that you want to break, make sure that you write down everything you can about it and make sure that you actually physically write it down on paper. Thinking about the cycle in your mind is simply not enough for you to be able to effectively see what your cycle is and then work through it. You need to be able to view it on paper. When you have it on paper, knowing and becoming aware of all of the details is a lot easier because you can actually, you know, *see* what is going on.

Identify Your Outcomes

Right now, your outcome is obviously anxiety, and that is obviously a problem. Clearly, you do not want to be experiencing anxiety anymore which is why you are reading this very book (duh!) So, we know that your unwanted outcome is experiencing anxiety. Now, you need to identify what your preferred outcome would be, like, you know, not experiencing anxiety. You can get as specific as you want with this outcome. Maybe, it's simply that you do not want to experience anxiety anymore, or it could be that instead of anxiety, you want to experience joy, positivity, happiness, or something else instead. Write down your desired outcome so that you know what it is that you are trying to achieve when you are breaking your anxiety cycle using CBT.

Now that you know what you want to achieve, you need to see how your current dysfunctional cycle is totally screwing up your outcome so that you can discover where your best opportunity to make a change is going to be. Your dysfunction likely arises in the thought process, where your poor brain seems to think that everything is trying to kill you or hurt you, so pay close attention to this part. You may also find that your physical responses to things are causing a problem, too, as you begin tensing up and physically responding with anxiety to random life events. In this case, your biofeedback, or the feedback your body is giving your mind, is telling you that you need to be anxious which is causing your anxiety to flare up.

After you have identified everything that is lending to your unwanted outcome, you can thank yourself for a job well done and start focusing on new strategies to whip yourself into shape. Ideally, you want to focus on shifting your thoughts and your physical responses. By overriding your automatic thoughts with conscious ones that serve you, and by choosing to change your physical posture when you are experiencing fear or anxiety, you actually set yourself up for what is known as "breaking state." In other words, you kick your keester out of the deer-in-the-headlights response, and shift into a more conscious, intentional, and appropriate response that actually helps you feel confident and capable of facing whatever it is that you are going through.

Challenge Your Thoughts

The next part of CBT happens when you are actually experiencing the anxiety, which can make this part of the process a bit harder. This is where a lot of people may get the wrong idea: no, I know you cannot always just "think positive" and get your way through a bout of anxiety, and anyone who attempts to tell you that is the be-all end-all solution has clearly never experienced the mind-crushing effects of anxiety itself.

What I am saying here is that you need to be willing to actually identify where your thoughts are likely false during a bout of anxiety or panic, and start trying to use logic to work your way through this moment of anxiety so that you are no longer being crushed underneath it. So maybe you can't simply think positive, but you can begin to challenge your thoughts by asking yourself whether or not they are actually true.

Challenging your thoughts typically works like this: first, you identify the problematic thought that is making you anxious. For example, "I cannot possibly get through this." Next, you need to ask yourself if this thought is inherently true, which in most cases it will not be. If it is not, you want to look for all of the evidence as to why you would be able to get through this and why you do not need to be worried that you are going to be somehow unable to get through this experience. Perhaps you think you cannot because you do not have the skills so you can begin to look for evidence that you can learn the skills. Or, maybe you think that you cannot because you are too scared so your body will not work for you because you are frozen with fear, in which case you can start looking for ways to relax your body so that you can begin feeling comfortable within your body again.

If the answer to your question is yes, that your fear is true, then you need to start looking at what the likely outcome is if your fear plays out. The best question to ask yourself here is: "then what?" So, if you decide that you cannot actually do something, then you ask yourself, "Then what?" and you realize that maybe the next part of the thought is, "Well, then I would need to learn the skill so that I could do it." Then, you may ask yourself again, "Then what?" so you realize "Well, then I could do it, and it would no longer be a problem."

That was a quick example, but sometimes the chain of thoughts may be longer, and sometimes it may be just as short, sweet, and simple as that. Seeing your fears all the way through to the outcome, rather than getting caught in the hardest part, is the best way to allow yourself to see that even if your fears do come true, in most cases you are going to be perfectly fine. This is a great way for you to start digging deeper into your problem-solving skills so that you can stop being overwhelmed by the crap that you have been telling yourself until now.

Replace Your Automatic Thoughts

In addition to challenging your thoughts, you also need to start replacing your automatic thoughts, because clearly, they are defective, and they've got you twitching out. Replacing your automatic thoughts comes from intentionally modifying and developing triggers for yourself so that when you see or experience something, the automatic thought that is produced is in some way helpful to minimize or eliminate your anxiety. You can recreate your automatic thoughts around your existing experiences, or you can create new automatic thoughts around completely meaningless triggers so that these triggers now become positive ones for you.

This starts with choosing what you want your new thought to be and then intentionally and repetitively thinking that new thought any time your trigger arises so that you eventually make it automatic. So, if you are trying to reprogram a thought response to a trigger, you may begin to think that your trigger is neutral and has zero impact on you. You can consciously continually think, "That does not affect me in any way," over and over every single time you see that trigger until your brain begins to automatically think, "That does not affect me in any way," any time your previous trigger is experienced.

If you are trying to program a new trigger, you can pick your object of choice and begin intentionally thinking something around that object every time you see it. For example, maybe you have a ring that you wear that you want to symbolize strength and courage—so every time you look at it, you think, "I am strong and courageous." By consciously and intentionally thinking this thought about the ring every time you see it, eventually this thought becomes automatic and any time you see your ring, you are going to think that and feel better about yourself, and eventually, you'll find yourself feeling better even without the ring.

You can turn anything into a trigger, and you can reprogram any trigger that you want to using repetitive thought processes. Naturally, programming something new will be easier than reprogramming something traumatic, so keep that in mind while being gentle and patient with yourself and managing your expectations. Do not expect yourself to suddenly stop shitting your pants every time you see a yellow monkey mascot simply because one time you decided to think a new thought around it. Sure, you may feel better at the moment, but if you're really early in your CBT journey, you should still pack an extra pair of underwear *just* in case you are caught off guard. Over time, your repetitive thoughts however, will become your automatic thoughts—that's how the negative thoughts got there in the first place. But until you find yourself completely neutral or unmoved by old triggers, do not ignore the fact that you may still have unwanted responses from time to time.

Review Your Cycle

After you have worked on creating your new cycle and have spent time invested in actually giving it an honest effort, you want to start reviewing it to see what you can do to improve it further. Reviewing your cycle is how you can ensure that your improvements are actually working and that you are experiencing the positive impact that you want to be having on your life. You can ensure that you are catching any hiccups along the way, that your improvements are effective and lasting, and that you are going to be able to continue moving forward in the right direction. If you are seeking to change multiple behaviors, reviewing your cycles on the present behaviors you are working on can help you determine whether or not you have made enough improvements to allow you to advance towards working on new patterns altogether.

You can work on reviewing your cycles in the same way that you identified them in the first place: start by paying attention to the behaviors and the outcomes surrounding the situation that you are working towards shifting. Then, pay attention to what emotions are existing around those behaviors and whether or not they are shifting or at least becoming more manageable. Understand that shifting your behaviors with CBT does not guarantee that you will no longer feel emotions of fear, anxiety, overwhelm, stress, or anything else, but instead means that you will have an easier time coping with these feelings. These feelings are unavoidable, as everyone experiences them to one degree or another from time to time. However, they can be managed in a more effective way to ensure that you can feel them without being overtaken or crippled by them.

Identify the behaviors and feelings, then identify what thoughts you are having in response, and how those thoughts are impacting you. If you are having thoughts about your environment that would clearly lead to distress, such as if you are fixating on unlikely dangers or threats, then you know that your thoughts are not yet shifting enough to allow your behavior to shift fully. In this circumstance, you need to continue working towards identifying and addressing your automatic thoughts so that you can continue creating that shift in your emotional and physical responses to your environment. As you continue reviewing your cycles, chances are you will find that you are doing way better at remaining calm and you are no longer getting your knickers in a knot over every little thing.

CHAPTER 20

ACCEPT IT

HAVE you ever been told that you just need to accept things as they are, and that's that? Listen, being told to "just get over it" is probably the number one way to piss someone off, and rightfully so. However, this is actually the entire basis of a particular therapy style that has actually proven to be highly effective in helping people chill out and stop getting so worked up over the little things in life. The key here is that you need to learn to get over things with compassion and in a way that is actually complete. You need to learn how to not only accept things, but also move forward with acceptance, rather than repressing things or living in a constant state of resistance around the experiences that you are having in your life. When you learn how to accept the things that are happening around you, getting your chill on becomes a lot easier.

The type of therapy I'm talking about is Acceptance and

Commitment Therapy (ACT). It can be approached in two ways: a psychological way, or a mindful way. If you are approaching ACT in a mindfulness way, that is great! However, pure mindfulness is not always enough for some people, as they need more in the way of psychological support and understanding when it comes to healing their mental wellbeing. Fortunately for you, the psychological approach is what I'm all about because it can be more prone to getting people results, so ACT may be just the thing for you.

How ACT Works

ACT works by educating people on how to have healthier coping strategies to use towards painful emotions and emotional experiences. In society and in school, we are not taught how to manage our emotions effectively. We are taught about parallelograms and the power of X squared, but we are not taught about our emotions and how they impact our bodies and minds, and what we can do about it. As a result, when it comes to emotional management, we often find ourselves attempting to push away or suppress our more disturbing emotions because they are painful or because they have been known to lead to negative outcomes. For example, maybe when you are stressed, you get angry—and when you are angry, you say things you regret. Hence, you attempt to control the situation by repressing your anger and your stress. Of course, this never works out in the long run because you end up even more stressed and irritable, but we lead ourselves to believe that it will be effective and we continue the behavior.

With ACT, your goal is to learn how to accept the emotions that you are experiencing, without attempting to manipulate or change them. Your goal here is not to attempt to rewire your values or your beliefs or to try to change your mind about anything, but instead to simply allow yourself to have these experiences and see them through. In the hippy-dippy explanation, all you are doing is becoming mindful and allowing yourself to go through your natural responses to the situation at hand. The psychological explanation to this is that you are allowing your body to naturally complete the process of the emotions that you are experiencing so that you are no longer repressing them and holding on to them deep inside of you.

When we experience emotions, our bodies literally turn into emotional machines: hormones and chemicals are produced and released, those trigger certain responses in the body, and the body jumps into action accordingly. For example, with happiness, dopamine and serotonin are produced, which then move through the brain and produce feelings of happiness, which can lead to responses like a gentler posture, or laughter. When you let your body complete the process of emotional responses by allowing emotions to happen, it allows your system to use up all of the hormones or chemicals it has created to produce that emotional response, which prevents you from bottling it up. This way, you can thoroughly release your emotions and move on. This sounds way better than the unsuccessful attempt at repression, which only leads to more negative emotions and more drama within you and also the lives of people around you.

ACT works through a three-step process: One—accept your current situation, Two—choose your direction, and Three—take action. As you continue to reinforce these three steps, they begin to work themselves into your psyche as being a memorized strategy for managing challenging emotions, which means that over time, your Emotional Intelligence Quotient (EQ) will grow.

Accept Your Current State

The first step with ACT is accepting your current state, which must happen before you move forward with any other step. I'm not talking the "yeah, yeah, yeah, I get it" type of acceptance either. I mean, you need to truly accept where you are at and stop beating yourself up over it, since you are not doing yourself any favors by treating yourself like chopped liver.

Accepting your current state means that you are no longer going to bully yourself or judge yourself for how you are feeling, nor are you going to attempt to push yourself to feel any differently than you already do, because you are safe to feel the way that you feel. When you accept your emotions, rather than intensifying the level of discomfort that you feel by also trying to deny your experience, you simply allow your energy and emotions to run their course. What ends up happening is that you realize that emotions like anger and stress are a lot less scary or overwhelming than you thought they were, because the bigger issue was from trying to deny those feelings rather than the feelings themselves.

Accepting how you feel also comes with a commitment to a specific method for approaching what you are going through. See, if you were not accepting how you felt, you would probably jump into unfortunate action on an impulse, and regret basically every single decision you made after that point following the inception of said emotion. For instance, if you were not accepting of your anger, you may explode and blame everyone else for how you were feeling, which would lead to worse emotions...and probably fewer friends. This type of behavior shows that you are resisting your anger in the first place, and gives you even more reason to resist your anger as you begin to believe that you are incapable of experiencing anger without becoming a douchebag as a result.

When you accept where you are, you can slow down and begin to learn how to respond to your situations as opposed to reacting to them so that your decisions are more effective and respectful. This is a great way to use your logical mind in conjunction with your primal emotions to create a sort of power couple that allows you to feel things, produce energies and emotions within your body, and then use that energy and those emotions to produce a desired outcome. You can do this by simply using your brain. Easier said than done, though, right?

At the end of the day, you need to be willing to accept your weaknesses, accept that you are not great at everything, accept how you feel and that sometimes your feelings are crummy, and to acknowledge that sometimes life sucks and you cannot escape it or change it. As you begin to accept these things—I mean really actually accept them and see them for what they are—you can stop defaulting to your douchebag setting, or any other setting that you are displeased with, and start responding to your emotions intentionally.

Choose A Valued Direction

Accepting your emotions and experiences is only one part of the solution, but do not forget that ACT entails a three-fold strategy for you to use when it comes to managing difficult feelings. The next step after accepting your emotions and experiences is to decide what you are going to do about them, as clearly you are going to need to have some form of resolution to help you release those emotions. If your feelings are being triggered by something ongoing, your resolve needs to include you finding a way to manage or put an end to that ongoing trigger so that you can stop experiencing those unwanted emotions.

For example, if your roommate is a total slob and you are sick of playing housewife to a grown adult, and you are sick of fighting over who needs to do the dishes this time, you need to come up with an actual resolve to this problem. Continuing to vent to your bestie about how much your roomie sucks doesn't count. First, you need to accept that you are angry and overwhelmed and that you are fed up with fighting with your roommate.

Then, you need to accept that your roommate is probably not going to automatically change so you are going to need to find a new resolve for how you are going to navigate this situation. Your resolve is where you are choosing what it is that you want to do about the situation that is going to allow you to honor your emotions and work through them without making them worse. In the roommate situation, this may include holding your roommate accountable by making a chore chart, or even moving out and finding a more respectful and organized roommate to live with so that you are no longer feeling uncomfortable or overwhelmed.

When you are choosing what direction it is that you will be moving forward with, you want to make sure that you are choosing a direction that you value. This is the big key between switching from reaction to response: reactions are impulsive and not thought through, and responses are thought through and reflect your values and your needs. Responding to something means that you took the time to actually figure out what you wanted and what you were trying to accomplish so that you can take action toward those desired accomplishments.

One situation where choosing a valued direction forward can be challenging is if you actually have no idea as to what it is that you value. It sounds strange, but many people haven't got a single clue as to what their core values are in life, which can make moving forward in alignment with their values pretty freaking difficult. Finding out what you value is a key first step in helping you move out of your sticky situation and find your way forward through challenging situations and emotions.

It is important to understand that sometimes, your core values in a given situation may differ from your overall core values. If you find that your general core values do not add up to make any degree of sense whatsoever in the situation that you are facing, it may behoove you to identify your core values *for that circumstance*. If you are pissed at your dimwitted boss and you value financial security, instead of ditching your job and vowing to denounce the economic system and never make a single dollar again, a better choice is to get a different job or start an online business that allows you greater financial security.

Take Action

After you have thought it through and committed to a decision that you feel aligns with your values and needs, *then* you can start taking action on your decision. It is still a good idea to move slowly with your action, especially if you are new to responding to overreacting, to ensure that you are moving through the response in the way that you intend to. Slowing down to choose a response and then flying through it with reactivity-based energy is only going to lead to you doing what it was that you were trying to avoid in the first place.

At first, this reactive tendency may be somewhat inevitable as your psyche is so used to responding this way, but ideally, in time, the more you slow it down and approach your emotions with intention, the easier it will be to shift into responsive mode instead. Over time, your brain will rewire itself, and those reactive cycles will be terminated in favor of ones that effectively support you in growing through your emotional immaturity. Through this, your emotional intelligence will increase—and you will find that managing things like stress, overwhelm, anxiety, and other unwanted or challenging emotions becomes a heck of a lot easier.

If you find that you are a highly reactive person, it may be beneficial to combine ACT with CBT, as different triggers of differing severities may benefit from one therapy style over the other. Just review your chosen responses to certain emotions in advance so that you have a general idea as to what it is that you want to do. In this case, you do not necessarily need to look at a specific behavior as you would in CBT to help you decide what it is that you are going to do in response to that behavior, but instead you can look at a specific emotion.

Consider an emotion that often overwhelms you and has you flying off the handle, and choose in advance how you can respond to this emotion differently. Perhaps, when you feel stress, you immediately shut down and begin plowing your way through everything on your to-do list, which inevitably leads to lots of mistakes, causing more stress and frustration. In this case, your goal would be to stop shutting down whenever you experience stress so that you can choose to respond to that particular stress in a better way. Choosing how you will respond to specific emotions using ACT practices is effective in helping you have a somewhat blanketed response to your feelings so that when they are triggered, you already have a better way of responding in place and ready to go. Since many times our emotions can be triggered unexpectedly or with not so obvious triggers, having this type of generalized choice put in place ahead of time can be helpful.

Review Your Choices

After you have gone through the process of developing, processing, and releasing an emotion, just like with CBT, you should always take some time to review. So be sure to re-examine your new choices and reflect on how well you did with managing the challenging emotion. When you are not used to having to manage your emotions, it can be easy for you to think that your results were much different than they actually were, depending on your level of confidence in yourself. You may find yourself lying to yourself and believing that you did better than you actually did, or you may find yourself lying to yourself and believing that you did worse. Either way, you are not honestly reflecting on your experience, and if you're not evaluating yourself based on truthful results, it's going to make it a lot harder to actually change.

Reviewing your choices does not have to be a challenging or lengthy process. All you need to do is sit down with a journal and write down what happened when you started experiencing the emotion, how you handled it, and what the resolution was. Don't skip the process of writing it down. Just find a way to make it easier or faster if you have to. If you want, you can keep everything in bullet points so that you are not writing anything out in long-form.

But keep consistent and honest records. You don't want to botch your memory up and lie to yourself. Writing it down as soon as possible after it happens keeps it right there on paper and holds you accountable for how things really went. This means that if you did not handle it well, you have something to look at that helps you understand why and that holds you accountable so that you can work towards doing better in the future. If you did handle it well, seeing it on paper stops you from being able to bully or underestimate yourself, and you can start seeing how pretty freaking awesome you are, after all.

You do not need to reflect on every single emotional experience you ever have, just the emotions that are causing negative outcomes or experiences for you. And be honest. The only person who needs access to this information is you so that you can develop a greater self-awareness around what it is that you are doing and whether or not it is effective. Any time you go through a particularly daunting or challenging emotional experience, or any time you are trying to transcend a continual unwanted reaction to difficult emotions, this journaling and reflecting can be super helpful. But don't feel obligated to create a minute-by-minute emotional play-by-play of each and every day of your existence.

CHAPTER 21

GET EXPOSED

ANYONE WHO HAS EVER SAID "DOING the same thing over and over and expecting different results is insanity" has obviously never heard of Exposure and Response Prevention Therapy (ERP). ERP therapy is what it sounds like: you expose yourself to a trigger over and over again until you stop being triggered by said thing because your brain finally starts to have a healthy response in place of an unhealthy one.

The key with ERP is to understand that the goal here is not to flood your brain with overwhelming emotions and force it to cope. In fact, doing it this way could result in you having a nervous breakdown and experiencing greater trauma or stress around your trigger. Or it could otherwise just cause a seriously adverse reaction to the whole ordeal. Attempting to King Kong your way through by pounding your chest and charging headfirst into what terrifies you or overwhelms you could just lead to you being crushed under crippling stress and anxiety. So if you value your mental health, I'd skip the King Kong route.

Instead, ERP is done by giving you some time to accumulate a tolerance towards the thing that usually sets off your anxiety. Over time, you increase that tolerance, and it stops terrifying the crap out of you, which allows you to be exposed to the trigger and have a neutral response instead of an overwhelmed one. When it comes to anxiety, using ERP is largely focused on helping you manage anxiety as an emotion, as well as manage any triggers that may lead to you having an overwhelming amount of anxiety in response to what you are going through.

How ERP Works

ERP works by adding a layer on top of CBT so that you can go a step further towards overcoming your most significant triggers that cause particularly challenging bouts of anxiety. If you are someone who has allowed for a significant amount of stress to build up and take over in your life, or if you are suffering from bigger or longer episodes of anxiety around certain triggers, ERP can help you go the extra mile in pulling those suckers out at the roots. ERP is generally lead by trained professionals for people who are dealing with OCD and similar levels of anxiety, so you best believe that this technique can work wonders on the anxiety that you are dealing with as an average human with slightly above average stress in your life.

ERP works by seesawing back and forth between building

up your coping skills and exposing you to your triggers so that you are able to manage them better with your new coping skills. The more you are exposed to your triggers and have positive (or at the very least neutral) responses, the more you are going to find those triggers to be easy to navigate as they arise in the future. Over time, you will have exposed yourself to the triggers so many times that they lose their power and their ability to turn you into a ball of bawling mush every time you are around them. Think of your ERP goal as getting in there and ripping out the weeds that are not serving you.

Get To Know Your Triggers

The first step in digging into ERP is getting to know your triggers, since you need to have an idea of what it is that you are targeting before you just go in with your guns blazing.

Finding your triggers might be easy and straightforward. If every time your disapproving and perpetually disappointed mother calls you, you start to feel your throat closing and your heart racing, chances are your mother is one of your triggers. Likewise, if every time you want to get on the bus to go to work you feel like the bus is closing in around you and the people are all looking at you like you are crazy, chances are that the bus or crowded spaces are your triggers. If you can easily identify what it is that's setting you off, get a journal, and write it down at the top of a blank page, and you'll use that as your starting point.

If your triggers are not as obvious to you, they don't immediately come to mind, or you otherwise cannot seem to identify them right off the bat, no problemo. You can use trigger journaling as a way to find the issue. This essentially means that you bring a journal around with you for a few days and write down every single anxious episode you have, what time it happened, and what happened immediately before that episode began. You can also consider jotting down notes about other details that are known to impact anxiety, such as how rested you felt and how hungry you were. So be sure to add in little details about your physical, mental, or emotional state at the time leading up to the trigger as well. Seeing as how this is the 21st century, you can of course use your phone to do this, but there's still something about physical pen and paper. A couple of days of journaling should give you a pretty strong understanding of what your triggers are, as you will begin to notice consistent patterns that make it obvious to you.

Ideally, you should be using a trigger journal regardless of whether or not you already know your triggers, as you are going to want to write down what your intensity level was around your triggers each time. If you have a trigger that constantly produces ultra high levels of anxiety and always seems to end in you feeling like a nuke just detonated right in front of your face, or even worse, leaves you feeling like you *were* the nuke that just detonated, you know that's a rough one, and you need to pay close attention to that trigger so that you can really work on it.

And here's another reason why a trigger journal is useful even if you already know what it is that sets you off. If you have a trigger that fluctuates, you'll want to look at it closer and consider what is contributing to it sometimes being worse than other times. What's different in each circumstance? How are you different in each circumstance as far as your state of mind or body? Digging into and analyzing these details will give you the information you need to nip this problem in the bud. Also, upon closer analysis, you may find that a particular issue is not the true trigger but is instead merely *related* to the true trigger. But either way, the insight you gain from a detailed trigger journal will prove super useful in your journey to healing.

Build Your Fear Ladder

Now that you have your triggers tracked and you are clear on how much of an anxious wreck you actually are, you need to start building what ERP therapists call a "fear ladder." Essentially, the fear ladder is a tool that you are going to use that will help you determine where you need to start working on your anxiety and what steps you need to take to get to where you want to go. In simpler words, you want to place your fears on a list, ranking them from least to most scary so that you can get an idea for what it is that is causing you to feel a little nervous versus what is causing you to almost literally crap your pants every time it comes up.

Your fear ladder is going to help you determine where your worst triggers are and if there are any overarching fears that you need to consider. For example, if you are afraid of crowded buses, busy malls, and full waiting rooms, your fear may not be the particular places, so much as the number of people standing around you while you wait. You don't have a bus issue, or a waiting room issue—you have a too-many-people issue. Malls for you are fine... as long as there are no people in them. Once you uncover something like this, you'd still want to do the work on the places, but you can also use ERP to work on being less anxious around boatloads of people.

As you're writing your fear ladder, it may not always be obvious how to rank everything. If you get to two of your fears, and it's looking like a tie, and you're having a hard time determining which order to rank them in, look at each trigger, and think about whether the actual physical experience of it bothers you, or the thought of it bothers you. If simply *thinking* about something makes you feel like you are having a coronary, that one should probably be ranked higher on the list and is going to require some more work from you.

Climb That Ladder

Now that you have your ladder created, you are going to want to start climbing that thing! When it comes to ERP, there are two ladders you are going to climb: the ladder of each specific fear, and the overall ladder. Keeping yourself well-paced and in check for the entire process is going to make sure that you are not overwhelming yourself and creating your own misery by trying to jump up the ladder like Mario and Yoshi super bouncing into the clouds. That way, you can set yourself up to have neutral or positive experiences with each trigger, rather than traumatizing yourself and making your anxiety ten times worse.

To climb the ladder effectively, start with your first fear

and then look at how afraid you are with that particular fear. If you are a 2 out of 10 for example, you know that you have fear around it, but that you are probably not going to pass out over it if exposed to it in any way. It may bring a high level of discomfort for you that makes you want to escape, but not quite jump off a cliff. This is a good base level of fear to start with. Now that this fear is identified, you want to decide what your coping strategies are going to be *before* you go into the situation that involves your fear. Having your strategy already planned means that you are far less likely to engage in your old behaviors when your fear is triggered because you can consciously remember what it is that you want to do when you get into the unnerving situation.

Each time you get into a fearful situation, set the intention to respond with your new effective strategies and not the old ones that made you quiver like a newborn giraffe. If you find that you are getting overwhelmed or that it's getting to be too much, do your best to walk away or end it so that you are not reinforcing even worse reactions. Overexposing yourself can put you in backward motion, so...don't do that. Instead, focus on healing yourself in a consistent, yet methodical manner so you can continually build up your tolerance towards your trigger until it stops triggering you altogether.

Once you have had success in overcoming a fear, you can move on to the next one on your ladder, and so on and so forth until you have worked through all of your triggers and you are a completely fearless badass in complete and total control over yourself...or at least something closer to that. Be patient, as many triggers may take a significant amount of time for you to work through, and some will take longer than others, especially if you're not going the King Kong overexposure route, so try to avoid rushing it, and be kind to yourself. Also, remember, pro tip is to start at the bottom of the ladder with the easier triggers, as you are not only building up your tolerance to those, but you are building up your tolerance to discomfort and anxiety in general. The more that you can build up your tolerance to these feelings in general, the easier it becomes for you to manage your more challenging triggers that are higher up the ladder, and the easier it becomes for you to manage unexpected uncomfortable situations that inevitably pop up in life in the future.

Rate Your Success

As per usual, once you have completed your ERP practice for a trigger, you want to take a moment to reflect and see if you have actually been successful or not. You may be able to tell right away, or you may want to begin writing down how exposure to each trigger feels each time to get a real-time view of how strong you are with the things that have a tendency to set you off. If you find that certain fears are no longer bothering you and that you have neutralized them, you can move on to the next one. If you find that you are still struggling, even though it may sound counterintuitive, you might want to try slowing down. Sometimes, pacing yourself and taking it easy can lead you to success faster because you are not pushing yourself forward so hard.

Let's say you get anxiety every time you drive a car, so every time you see a car, that fear is triggered within you and your heart starts beating out of your chest and your hands shake. Instead of jumping straight behind the wheel and going on a cross country road trip, start with baby steps, taken consistently over time. Maybe Day 1, you just look at the car for as long as you can stand. Day 2, you get in, but sit in the passenger seat. Day 3, you sit in the driver's seat and buckle up. Day 4, you start the car, but keep it parked. Then over time, you gradually start driving for longer and longer distances. Or maybe you start off having someone ride with you and work your way up to driving alone.

So if you're having a difficult time with a fear, think of how you could break down your exposure in a similar way. You want to allow yourself to acclimate to changes over time. If you find that you have put in a lot of effort and you are really struggling, you may be dealing with above average levels of anxiety which may require more support than just a self-help book. In that case, never be afraid to consult a professional to seek help. Sometimes doing everything on your own can be too challenging, and having compassionate and professional support on your side can be more effective with getting you to where you need to go.

PART 5

DOING THE WORK & MAKING LASTING CHANGE

CHAPTER 22

DEAR DIARY

THROUGHOUT THIS ENTIRE BOOK, there are references to using a journal or a diary as a way for you to work through your anxious feelings and start feeling relief from the symptoms that you have been experiencing. When it comes to dealing with anxiety, having a pain diary can help you in a number of different ways, so keeping one handy is a great opportunity for you to start overcoming your struggles. Now, understand this—a daily pain diary does not have to be something you gush in about your crush, nor do you need to complain about Bob from Accounting's weird mouth breathing or anything like that. You do not need to use this particular diary to document every little element of your life and everything you are feeling and experiencing.

Instead, use it to focus directly on experiences related to your healing. You can use your diary in any format that feels right for you—whether that be jotting down a few sentences, filling it out in bullet points, or adding several pages worth of information that comes up for you throughout the day. There is no right or wrong way to use this tool, as long as you are willing to use it on a regular basis to get your thoughts and notes out on paper so you can actually begin to see patterns, draw conclusions, and evaluate progress. The more that you are willing to use it, the more you will be able to develop your self-awareness around your anxiety and start feeling confident in yourself, leaving your anxious responses to begin to subside over time.

Let's explore a handful of different ways that you can use your pain diary to help you get things out of your mind, identify what you are working on, and give you a realistic idea of what you need to be working through. You may choose to use one of the following methods or all of them. The choice is yours.

Daily Thought Log

Using a daily thought log can be a great opportunity for you to see where your thoughts are getting the best of you and how they may be causing problems for you in your day-to-day life. It is important to go deeper into your thoughts, as your words and emotions are not always going to be a clear reflection as to how you are doing on a daily basis. Sometimes, we may feel like we are doing better than we actually are because our mood has not yet caught up to the underlying thoughts that we are having subconsciously, or we are so used to having a stressed out mood that we do not recognize it as being abnormal.

Allowing yourself to have a daily thought log helps you see how you are feeding your brain, and what you are telling yourself on a consistent basis.

If you use your pain diary as a thought log, be sure to use it as both a log that tracks your negative and problematic thoughts, and a log that tracks your positive and helpful thoughts. You want to get clear on both how you are hindering yourself and how you are helping yourself so that you can see where your thought patterns lie and how they are affecting your overall wellbeing.

Finding your negative thought patterns is going to help you see where you are causing your anxiety to grow worse so that you can prevent this from happening any further. Finding your positive thought patterns is going to help you see where you are supporting yourself so that you can be more compassionate toward yourself in general and see what thoughts to reinforce. It is always a good idea to balance out your self-awareness by looking at both your negative and positive traits so that you do not feel like you are a complete failure at this being a human being thing. This will help you keep everything in perspective, and will give you a foundation upon which you can start building more positive or helpful thought patterns.

Anxiety Outbursts Log

Another type of log you can keep in your daily pain diary is one that tracks how many times you have difficulty with anxiety in your daily life. Write down every time your anxiety grows noticeable, and be sure to keep details about what has caused it to get this way so that you can begin to have a greater awareness as to how your anxiety functions.

When you do write down your anxiety outbursts, note things like:

- The time of day
- Your current state (how rested you are, when you ate, what you ate if you feel your food is impacting your anxiety, etc)
- The severity of your anxiety on a scale of 1-10, with 1 being no anxiety (in which case, you wouldn't be writing anything down) and 10 being the worst anxiety
- The trigger that caused your anxiety (whether person, place, thing, event, or a combination)
- Thoughts that you were having
- Physical symptoms you were having
- Coping methods that you tried
- What coping method worked

This way, you have a very detailed log that allows you to understand the nature of your anxiety and how your anxious outbursts or mild panic attacks, are impacting you throughout your daily life. The more detailed your log is, the easier it is for you to navigate an anxious experience in the future because you have a clearer sense of what is making you anxious, how your anxiety feels, and what works when it comes to coping with and releasing it.

Accountability Log

Accountability logs are another great tool that you can implement when it comes to daily pain diaries. Many people claim that they are willing to make a difference when it comes to dealing with their anxiety (or anything in life really), but they go on to find themselves not actually *doing* anything about it. You may buy this book and twelve others, read all of them, nod your head at how genius the ideas seem, or lament about how much they suck and don't work, meanwhile, instead of implementing anything, you're continuing to do all the same crap that has your panties in a bunch in the first place. Seems silly, but as we all know, things like this happen *all* the time.

If this sounds like you, first off note that this is likely just a bad psychological pattern that you are using as a way to try to avoid what you need to do most—heal your anxiety. But don't beat yourself up over this. Instead, notice this pattern and include it as something that you want to heal when it comes to dealing with your anxiety so that you can begin healing yourself from your self-sabotaging tendencies, too. There's a double whammy for your pain diary.

Once you decide that it's actually time to take action if things are ever going to change, you can begin an accountability log in your pain diary, which essentially is a log where you hold yourself accountable for doing the work. In this log, you should write down when your anxiety happened and what tools you used to navigate your anxiety. This way, you are able to see how effective your work is, how much progress you are making on a consistent basis, and you are able to hold yourself accountable to actually making the changes that you desire to make.

"What's Bothering Me" Log

If you still have no clue as to why you are such an anxious little wreck, writing down what is bothering you on a regular basis can be a good way to find your triggers and understand why you are so bothered. A "what's bothering me" log is not necessarily devoted to triggers specifically, but it gives you space to just freely write down everything that is preventing you from feeling comfortable and calm at the moment. So maybe this can be your opportunity to vent and rant about Bob from Accounting's mouth breathing every time you pass his cubicle.

If you are feeling bothered or stressed out by things that happened to you in the past or by something you did a while ago, you can use this log to write about it and get it out of your mind. Sometimes, just getting something out on paper is plenty to help you deal with it and release it so that you can move on and grow forward through whatever has been bothering you. Other times, this will simply bring to the surface what you need to deal with so that you can find a focus point and appropriate strategy from which to start your healing process.

CHAPTER 23

THE MAGIC OF MEMORY

REMEMBER when I basically told you to get a grip on your reality and start owning and seeing your anxiety for what it really is? And remember when you wanted to backslap me for being so insensitive? Now, it is time that I give you another helpful tool to help you get a grip on your anxiety so you no longer have a reason to backslap me.

This tool is extremely simple, yet it works wonders in teaching your mind to turn down freak out mode, and start functioning normally. The tool revolves around relation and memories, and it has the potential to totally bust the butt of any anxious moment you have from here on out. Putting this tool to work in your own life can change everything for you, as long as you use it consistently and really devote to the practice of letting it sink in for you.

Your memory is a wickedly powerful tool, and it has the power to shape virtually everything for you in your life. That's because your memory is something that you own, something that you can hold on to indefinitely, and something that your brain already validates as being true and honest. Even when memories are wrong, your brain will believe in them and treat them as facts, making your emotions and actions respond accordingly...which means that you can totally swing this in your favor. That, my friends, is the basis of how you can use your memory to your advantage.

How Relating To Memories Works

Because your brain sees your memories as being factual information, you can actually tap into your memories and draw on specific information to essentially convince your brain that what you are thinking is true. Think of it this way: say one time in the past, your friend stole something from you, and your evidence of this was that they were suddenly avoiding you, and they would get angry and weird any time you attempted to go into a certain part of their house because that is where they were hiding the stolen goods. In your memory, it was the evasiveness and the aggression around their privacy that indicated that something was wrong, and so you now know this to be a red flag any time someone begins behaving in this way.

Now, let's say that you are in a new friendship and your new friend who you do not know very well seems to be evasive with certain pieces of information and perhaps tries to protect their privacy over certain areas of their home by not inviting you into those areas. To your new friend, they may just be avoiding sharing parts of their personal life with someone that they do not know very well. Perhaps they have not decided whether or not they trust you yet, so they are not ready to let you in completely until they have learned whether or not you can be trusted. Or maybe they're just not inviting you to certain areas of their house because they're not decorated, or not clean.

To you, however, this may scream "red flag" because this is exactly how your old friend behaved when they had stolen something from you. Even though your current situation is not the same because this new person has not stolen from you, your memory and your brain have decided that they have, and so you have convinced yourself that this person has something to hide. As a result, you may not trust this person, and the friendship may not work out because of how you have both behaved.

Your memory can serve as a benefit when you are avoiding certain dangers or unwanted situations, but it can also trigger false alarms and leave you on high alert in totally harmless situations. When this happens, it is called "relating to your memories" because you are relating your present experiences to your past ones, which helps you decide whether or not the present situation is safe for you to be in. In some situations, particularly when you are not consciously aware of what you are doing, relating to your memories can totally screw you over and leave you feeling like nothing is safe. However, when you use relating to your memories in a deliberate and intentional way, you can actually leverage this as a tool to teach your brain that you are totally fine and that there is nothing for you to be anxious about.

Relating To Memories With Anxiety

When it comes to relating to your anxiety-laden memories, you need to be willing to consciously step into the practice of identifying where your memories can serve you by showing yourself that the present situation is not as dangerous as you might think it is. For instance, say you have anxiety around being in someone's house at night because you watched too many scary movies growing up... or just because you are not used to being in unfamiliar places at night. But one night, you find yourself at a new friend's house for movie night, and they step out to run to the store and get some snacks, leaving you alone in an unfamiliar place at night.

Once they leave, it triggers your anxiety. You might find yourself having a hard time calming down because you think something bad is going to happen or that you are not safe because your brain is so unfamiliar with your surroundings. Of course, this is not necessarily the case, so here is a perfect opportunity to learn to relate to your memories in order to teach your mind that you are totally fine and you have nothing to worry about.

You can do this by remembering all of the times that you have been alone at night, and nothing happened. You were fine when you were alone at night at your own house. Nothing bad happened when you were alone at night at your sister's house. There have been countless times where you were alone in a house at night and nothing happened, so why would things automatically be any different at your new friend's place? They wouldn't. So you have nothing to worry about.

Often, in an anxious situation, your brain will not instinctively bring forth these memories because they were rather mundane, which is exactly why recalling on these lame, anticlimactic memories works so well. Nothing happened then, which means that you can convince your mind that nothing will happen now, because in all previous situations, you were totally fine and there was nothing for you to worry about.

Getting Your Mind On Board

As you convince your mind that nothing freaky is going to happen, you will start to feel your body respond. You'll begin to physically let go of any stress that you may have been holding on to that was preventing you from relaxing completely. And as this stress is released, so is your anxiety, all because you have convinced your mind that there is no reason for you to be stressed or afraid.

If you find that your mind is still struggling to get on board, chances are that you are questioning your memories or that you doubt that they are truly relevant to the situation. Or, you may find that you are countering your memories of safety and comfort with contrary thoughts that this time is the time that you will not be safe for whatever reason you have come up with. As you continue to come up with these thoughts that challenge the idea that you are safe, you want to make sure that you are also coming up with thoughts that challenge the idea that you are *not* safe. You can make a game out of it.

Decide that every time you come up with a reason for why this is the time that you are going to die, you will also come up with a reason for why this time is the same as all the others and you are totally safe and out of harm's way during this experience. That's the game. The prize is mental peace. Wanna play?

The more you continue to challenge your thoughts and use your memories to convince you that you are, in fact, safer than you think, the more you are going to find yourself letting go of the fears that you have around the present situation. Soon enough, fears will be diffused, and you will stop feeling like a total loose cannon at the worst possible time.

CHAPTER 24

DISOWN YOUR WEIRD UNCLE

NO MATTER what that brain of yours tries to have you believe, you are not your thoughts, and you will never be your thoughts. Your thoughts are simply tools that you use to perceive and interpret the world—nothing more and nothing less. Sometimes, your thoughts are totally accurate, and they serve you in having a true and positive experience of the world around you. Other times, your thoughts are hopped up on loco juice, and they are feeding you with crazy information that has you feeling crazy and thinking about all sorts of things that are irrelevant and unhelpful.

Everyone has that crazy uncle (usually perpetually hopped up on loco juice) who the family wants to disown. And if you don't think you have that crazy uncle, it's because you never met him because he was already disowned. Are you going to take life advice from your crazy, loco juice sipping uncle? No. Don't listen to everything your crazy uncle says. Don't listen to everything your thoughts say. Disown your crazy, loco juice sipping uncle. Disown your thoughts.

This is how you will detach from what you are thinking and stop identifying yourself with every single thing that pops into your head. This will allow you to consciously choose to interpret the world in a new way that actually serves you and helps you have a more positive experience of your life. When you find that you are having anxiety and your thoughts are not serving you, you can separate yourself from your thoughts as a way for you to stop engaging in your anxiety and start engaging in something more positive.

Any time you find yourself engaging in unhelpful thoughts—you want to disengage by either disowning the thoughts entirely or distracting yourself so that the thoughts no longer have control over your mind and emotions. Now, let's see how.

Identify Your Thoughts

You would think identifying your own thoughts would be easy, right? *Um, hello, they're those incessant, often nonsense words that I have running through my head all day long.* In most situations, it is easy to see what you are thinking: you simply want to start consciously becoming aware of the dialogue in your head and what it is telling you. However, sometimes gaining awareness of your thoughts is not all that simple. Because we spend so much time in our lives thinking, we are not always fully aware of *what* we are thinking. In many instances, we are not even aware of the fact that we *are* thinking at all. We just begin to have emotional and physical reactions that we may not even fully understand. This type of disconnect can be totally normal, yet it can also lead to unwanted situations that can make life a lot more challenging than it needs to be.

The best way to begin identifying your thoughts is to tune in any time you are having strange or unwanted physical or emotional reactions. If you start feeling your anxiety climb, slow down and tune in to your thoughts so you can get a handle on what you are thinking and what you are telling yourself. Pay attention to your current dialogue and, if possible, try to remember what your inner dialogue was just moments before you began having these feelings or responses.

Once you have identified the thoughts in your brain, you need to identify the problematic ones. This is the way to discover which of your thoughts are leading to anxiety and what they are saying to you so that you can begin to eliminate those thoughts. It is important for you to decipher which of these thoughts are actually problematic, and which are normal. You might think that any and every thought you are having around anxiety is problematic, but this is actually not true. Acknowledging your anxiety is totally fine, as is acknowledging the reason for your anxiety, as both of these discoveries give you the opportunity to deal with them, rather than becoming emotionally numb and never facing your truth. However, there will inevitably be some disempowering thoughts going on around your experience of anxiety. Those are the problematic ones we want to work through and eliminate.

If you are anxious about giving a presentation and you respond to that anxiety by repeating in your head "I can't do this, I can't do this..." over and over again, your thought of "I can't do this" is problematic and unhelpful, and will prevent you from moving forward and block you from finding a solution. If you were able to disown that disempowering thought instead of believing it, you would have the mental clarity to come to the conclusion that your anxiety can likely be greatly reduced or even overcome by preparing yourself for the presentation.

Disown Your Anxious Thoughts

Your thoughts are not your own. As much as you want to think that your beliefs, ideas, and thoughts are 100% original, everything that goes through your head is shaped by people, situations, and experiences outside of you, and most of it is from a long, long time ago. Your brain is full of borrowed thoughts—some positive, some negative, some helpful, some unhelpful. If you borrowed something —a movie back in the days of DVDs, a book back in the days of libraries, a shirt from your friend—and you didn't like it, you wouldn't use it, and would likely return it. You wouldn't force yourself to watch an entire crappy movie, read a whole 600 page crap book , or force yourself to wear an unflattering outfit. If it doesn't tickle your fancy, you don't use it. Same goes for your thoughts.

There is no rule that says you are required to hold on to every thought, even if it is not helpful. Whenever an unhelpful thought arises, practice saying, "This is not my thought, and I do not truly believe this thought to be true; therefore, I am disowning this thought now." Once you disown the thought, release it and set the conscious intention to no longer think about this idea, as it is not serving you in feeling any better overall. In some cases, this simple practice of consciously letting go of the thought is sufficient to help you move beyond it and start feeling better about yourself and everything that you are going through. In other cases, you may find that consciously disowning the thought is not enough and that you are still holding on to it, or it is still impacting you in some way. That's where this next step comes into play.

Choose New Thoughts

When simply removing your problematic thoughts is not enough, you need to choose new thoughts for you to think in place of the problematic ones. Look at it this way: your brain is an incredible supercomputer that has plenty of power to be able to do all types of different things at once, and it loves having a job to do. Your brain likes to be employed. But most of us just let our brains run wild like a rabid dog, doing whatever it wants, not stopping to consider what type of damage it may be doing or danger it may be causing in the process.

If your brain is like this, when you try to eliminate a negative thought, you are going to find your brain always filling up the gaps with automatic thoughts, which will likely also be influenced by your negativity bias—that archaic survival mechanism we have that causes a tendency to look for the negative in everything. This means that if you put in all of that effort towards eliminating unwanted anxious thoughts only to find yourself refilling the space with more anxiety, you are going to be extremely disappointed in yourself. This will keep you on an unwanted cycle of constantly making life harder for no good reason.

Instead of letting your brain do whatever it wants and run amuck like a poorly trained dog...or child...when you disown a disempowering thought, try filling the empty gap with a positive or productive thought that is going to help you actually move forward in a positive and productive way. At first, this can be challenging, especially if you are extra prone to negativity bias because you have yet to train your brain, but over time this will shift. You will find that if you are always feeding your mind with positive information, it is easier for you to continue thinking positive thoughts, naturally. So, get to work on feeding that brain of yours some good brain food!

Distract Yourself From Unhelpful Thoughts

In addition to disowning and replacing your negative thoughts, here's a different strategy if you need something else to help you completely release yourself from their grip —distraction. Distracting yourself from thoughts that are not supporting you with feeling better can be a great way to move beyond the pressure of trying to get yourself to think differently when your mind is being stubborn. Let's be honest, sometimes your mind is simply unwilling to get on board with what you are trying to do, and it is more than willing to throw itself on the ground and kick and scream like a toddler in their terrible twos.

If getting yourself on board with your new perspective is not working, completely switching your train of thought altogether can be a powerful way for you to stay focused on the good, and get yourself through a moment of anxiety.

Let's go back to our presentation example. Maybe the more that you try to think that you are going to be okay with getting on stage and giving that presentation, the more anxious you feel about having to do it. Although you are doing your best to get your mind to think right thoughts, you also find yourself coming up with as many different ways as possible that you can back out, cancel, or otherwise avoid having to do it. If this is the case, you need to distract yourself.

Distracting yourself is something that needs to be done sneakily. Many people attempt to engage in a distraction by doing something else, yet their mind is still being heavily occupied with what they are afraid of having to do. In this case, your distraction is as good as worthless because you are still winding yourself up—now, you are just keeping your hands busy while you do it. If you want to engage in a real distraction, you need to do something that is not only going to engage your body, but your mind, too. You need to find something that is going to draw your mind in and keep you distracted for as long as possible until you are no longer thinking about the thought that brought you anxiety.

If and when you do begin to think about what is bringing you anxiety again, monitor it to make sure that you are not engaging in the problematic thoughts. The moment you find yourself engaging in them once again, you can move back into distraction mode so that you are no longer overwhelmed by these thoughts. You can keep going back and forth until eventually, you find yourself thinking about that which is bringing you anxiety without having an actual overwhelming outbreak of anxiety from problematic thoughts. This way, you can begin to move forward more confidently and stop feeling like your anxiety is coming in and ripping the rug out from underneath you.

CHAPTER 25

FOR REAL, THOUGH?

LET'S talk about the difference between describing vs. evaluating. This essentially requires you to ensure that when you are judging a situation, you are judging it based off of the right information. See, as humans, we have a tendency to make observations, describe these things to ourselves, and make judgments and choose reactions based off of these descriptions. Of course, descriptions can be totally subjective, as your description could be based on your own past or present opinions, feelings, or perceptions towards what's happening in a specific situation.

A description, for example, could be that "there was an ugly sofa in the room." The sofa being considered ugly is just an opinion unique to you, as not everyone may see that sofa as being ugly. Although a sofa means nothing to your anxiety (hopefully), you can now see how describing things based off of your own opinions and thoughts about them can become problematic when you are combatting anxiety. Instead of *describing* things subjectively as we naturally tend to do, and getting swallowed up by the unpleasant implications of our own opinions, we can start learning how to *evaluate* things so that we can really get the actual facts into our minds. This way, at least your brain is being fed with the truth before you jump down the anxiety rabbit hole and start having a total meltdown.

Why Describing Leads To Anxiety

It's simple. I'll tell you why. Well, actually, I already did. As in the example above, your descriptions can be totally subjective and unhelpful. Let's talk about a hypothetical situation where you rely on descriptions instead of evaluations, and watch what the natural and realistic progression of your thought process can be when using descriptions.

Imagine you are standing in an alleyway (not off to a good start, are we?). A dog rounds the corner and starts walking towards you, and you need to quickly decide whether or not you are in danger because of this dog. Say the dog caught you off guard, and you definitely do not know this dog, so there is a valid element of uncertainty or surprise relevant in the situation. Your description might sound something like:

"Shit. There is a huge, scary dog walking down the alley toward me. I don't know this dog; it looks murderous, and it probably wants to kill me. Look, it's mouth is open, I bet it is sizing me up and getting ready to attack me. Its ears are pricked back. Probably a sign of hunger...or listening to make sure no one's coming to save me. It probably has

equally hungry and murderous dog friends who are going to come too. I am absolutely going to get attacked by this dog right now. And when it gets full and is finished with me, it'll signal to its friends to come finish my remains."

See how that story progressed from seeing a dog to feeling 100% confident that the dog was going to attack, ending the story with imminent death? With that description, you never stopped to look at the entire situation fully— therefore, you have not really come to understand whether or not you are truly in danger. Because you were describing the situation to yourself rather than evaluating it, you did not stop to look for important information such as how the dog was moving, if it was growling, or whether or not it actually looked or acted like it was going to attack. All of the important information was missed in this description, and you have already assigned meaning to what few clues you did observe, meaning that you have an incomplete and inaccurate, emotionally charged view of what is actually going on, and have caused yourself a heart attack before the dog even gets any closer to you.

Why Evaluating Leads To Peace Of Mind

If you were evaluating the above situation with the same dog, rather than fixating on the information that fit the description of your fears, you would look for the bigger picture. If you were *evaluating* a situation involving a strange dog walking toward you in an alleyway, you would explain the situation more completely. Your evaluation would likely sound something like:

"Whoa, there is a dog walking towards me. Okay. I

definitely do not recognize this dog, but I do not yet know if it is a danger or not. Its mouth is open, but it's panting, so I think it's just tired. His ears are pointing back, that could look concerning. Is he listening to something or is that just the relaxed position of his ears? It doesn't seem to be looking at me, so I do not think I am in danger as it does not seem to care that I'm here. Looks like it has a collar, so it's someone's pet and not a stray dog, so that's a good sign. I also don't hear any growling, so I don't think it feels angry or threatened. I am probably okay in this situation."

This time, you more thoroughly evaluated the situation and received all of the necessary information about it to make a reasonable, informed decision based on logic. You were still very much aware, alert, and observant during the situation, but by seeing things objectively and not automatically resorting to freak out mode, you didn't get yourself into an unnecessary state of anxiety over someone's pet dog. Instead, you were able to stay in control and make a clear-headed decision on what you were going to do.

Had you actually turned out to be in trouble, you at least would have been calm enough to make a choice that would be far more likely to protect you and keep you safe than if you had gotten yourself worked up and paralyzed in an anxious, frazzled knot. After all, we all know that we tend to make poorer decisions and exercise poorer judgment when we are worked up and feeling stressed out.

Switching Gears In Action

Alright, choosing to see things from a new light when

you're reading a book about a person in a hypothetical situation is one thing, but what about when you are actually in the situation? What if you *are* caught off-guard by a strange, growling dog, and your butt cheeks are clenched, and your back hairs are raised, and you are trying not to shit yourself? What then? How do you switch from description to evaluation when you are actively in the situation of feeling totally terrified and caught off-guard?

Like most things, the answer is simple on paper, but requires a little more effort in real life: you need to be willing to exercise willpower and override your knee jerk response. That's right—you need to identify your desire to stay safe and then make the executive decision that you will stay safer through evaluating the situation calmly than you will through describing it frantically. Then, without giving your brain time to argue, you need to begin evaluating the situation by asking yourself to identify all of the information about the situation that you possibly can.

As you are identifying the information, ask yourself this one very important question: "Is that the truth, or is that my opinion?" This way, you can hold yourself accountable for keeping the information that you are feeding yourself about any given situation true. After all, you would not want to be telling yourself false stories when you are attempting to regain control over that brain of yours. That would just be counterproductive.

Start this process now, with situations that are not potentially life threatening. In a potentially life threatening situation, you may not always have time to go through the clunky breakdown of different individual mental steps and questions to make sure you are evaluating properly. So I suggest you get in the habit now of observing the objective truth about situations so you can start to evaluate and not describe as second nature.

That way, if you do get into a situation that has higher stakes than just being pointed and laughed at, you've already exercised your evaluation muscles and it will be your habitual way of thinking and responding, so having a clear enough head to avert real danger will be much easier for you. Over time, as you continue to respond to overwhelming situations with evaluations rather than descriptions, you will find that it becomes far easier for you to choose the evaluation route by default, as you will be rewiring your brain to respond in a healthy and sensible way.

CHAPTER 26

YOU'RE FULL OF IT

YOU ARE a freaking genius when it comes to making shit up. Whether you think you are creative or not, you're a master at making up stories and telling them to yourself and to others. Telling stories is a fundamental tool in our modern language, which is why virtually every person is good at storytelling in some way or another. Telling stories does not mean that you are making up false information and telling lies, either. You are not Kelly at the water cooler, dishing out the dirt on all the coworkers every lunch break, knowing full well that most of what she is telling is completely fictional. Telling stories just means that you are communicating your experience with yourself or other people, and that you are doing a pretty darn convincing job of it, too.

That being said, there are certain stories that you are telling that *are* full of crap and that are totally screwing you up. Even the most honest among us tell lies to ourselves and others pretty damn easily, without even realizing it, and we do it all the time.

Here's a little example. Let's say you're out with someone, and you say something odd and immediately feel embarrassed about what you said. Now, you're telling yourself some story about how that person will no longer like you because of what you said, and how you have totally ruined your reputation, and that you are not worthy of having friends because you are a total moron so you should just go eat worms.

Of course, none of this is true, but you have thoroughly convinced yourself that it is, which now has you feeling like a total fool and now probably acting even more weird because you've convinced yourself of this story. What's worse is that the other person will likely never validate that none of this is true because they themselves have already forgotten about it, yet you find yourself using this as validation that they *are* upset and weirded out and that all of your crazy stories are in fact true. After all, it only makes sense, doesn't it? Surely if *you* are still hung up on it, they must be too, and them not talking about it is proof that they are so mad that they will probably never talk to you again, right? Wrong. This is just your brain at work, telling you crazy stories that are completely untrue and leading you to feel like a total psycho over it.

Other Crazy Shit You Tell Yourself

I'm not inside of your brain, but I have one myself, and I know how these things can tend to work from my own firsthand experience. I am willing to bet that you have a whole list of common stories running through your head. Maybe you tell yourself that you are not as attractive as other people, and therefore, you do not deserve to have certain things or be treated a certain way in life. Maybe you believe that your intelligence levels, income levels, gender, height, weight, attitude, social class, or address in one way or another define or limit who you are and what you get to be and have in life. Heck, you might even be telling yourself stories from childhood that have you believing that because you accidentally bumped into your friend in third grade, making them trip and fall down the stairs, that you're a klutz and a bad friend, and no one is safe around you. You're probably telling yourself a bunch of crazy shit.

We don't just tell stories about our pasts, either. No, we like to tell stories about our futures, too. In fact, we *love* telling stories about our futures. Like the story about how we will never get married, how we'll die alone, or how we will never get a better job, or never make more money than we're making right now. We might even tell ourselves stories about how when we go on that dinner date tonight, the person we are going out with will definitely not like us, and we'll faceplant on the sidewalk on the way to the restaurant entrance before we even get inside, and make a complete fool of ourselves before we can even check in at the host stand. Maybe you tell yourself stories like how if you were to go to the mall by yourself, you would fall down the escalator and need to go to the hospital, and every single person in the whole mall would stop whatever they're doing and point and laugh at you. Yeah, the stories are crazy and unfounded, but somehow you have convinced yourself to believe in them, and now, you cannot possibly get your mind back under control, right? Wrong. It's just time to revisit your storytelling skills so that you can rewrite your stories, my friend.

How You Can Rewrite Your Stories

Rewriting your stories probably seems too simple to be true. I mean, you take your stories that you are telling yourself now, you identify where you are totally wigging out, and then you rewrite that part of the story so that you are not freaking out anymore. That bit about going to the mall and falling down the escalator? Maybe instead, you rewrite the story so that you, you know, *don't* fall down the escalator and find yourself in the hospital for a freak accident. Maybe you help someone else who's about to fall down the escalator. Or maybe there's no escalator involved at all. There's no rule that says that every mall story has to include an escalator. Maybe you go to the mall and meet the love of your life in the food court. Maybe instead of convincing yourself that you'll spill a drink at the sandwich stand, triggering a resounding point and laugh by all present in the food court, you tell yourself that even if you did spill your drink, that it is very likely that no one would even see, or care. I mean really, why would anyone worry about a random slob at the mall? Do you really think that will be the highlight of their entire day? And if it is, don't you think that says more about them than about you?

Rewriting your stories is not that hard, and yet it can

totally change your perspective for the better on what did happen, or what will happen in your future. The more that you work toward writing better stories that actually make you the hero, or at the very least not the loser, the more you will find yourself enjoying a positive experience of your life. Now, instead of worrying that every little thing is going to be an opportunity for you to be turned into a meme or a viral YouTube video labeled "that idiot who did...fill in the blank," you can simply go out and enjoy the fact that you are a totally average person that no one really cares about. Doesn't that make you feel better? I mean, your parents and your friends totally love you, but that guy six tables away eating a pretzel? Let's be real, he does not give one crap about you, and that is actually pretty damn liberating.

Telling The Story Of Self-Acceptance And Self-Love

Try not to gag at this one, but really, telling yourself a story of self-acceptance and self-love is important when it comes to dealing with your anxiety. Chances are, if you're particularly crippled by anxiety, you are always going to have a tendency to find new things to worry about or new fears to write into your story. That's where self-acceptance and self-love come into play, as they are the foundation for the self-confidence and self-esteem that can make you just plain not care about what other people think. Think for a moment how much of your anxiety is rooted in what other people think of you. If you no longer cared what other people think, imagine how easily so much of your anxieties and fears would magically fizzle away.

When you tell yourself stories, try telling yourself that even if these seemingly horribly humiliating things did occur, you would still love yourself. This way, you can feel confident that even if you were to make a horrible fool of yourself and everyone was laughing and treating you like the latest exhibit at the zoo, you would still love yourself anyway. Sure, your ego and pride may take a little blow, but you would feel a lot more confident and at peace, knowing that you were going to have your own back and come out the other side loving yourself just as much as you always have. The more that you can affirm this to yourself, the better you are going to feel overall. In the end, it really doesn't matter what people think. Don't give someone else's opinion of you more weight than your own.

CHAPTER 27

GET A GRIP

LISTEN, your anxiety is just anxiety. Yeah, I know, if someone says that when you are clutching your chest and gasping for air while debating whether or not this is *just* anxiety, you probably want to punch them in the face. However, it is also important that you get a grip and put your anxiety into perspective if you are ever going to get a handle on it. Anxiety is often rooted in the *fear* that something will happen, the *thought* that something will happen—that thing that's making you anxious is *not actually* happening.

In a way, if you take yourself out of it, and zoom out of the experience, it's kind of like being in a virtual reality war video game and being shot at while bombs go off all around you. It can feel real when you're in it, but really, you're in no *real* danger, it just *feels* like you are. Letting yourself hold on to the idea that you are three seconds from the grave every time you see something that makes you uneasy is only going to make your anxiety worse. If you take a moment to realize that this is just anxiety that you are experiencing, not an actual threat, you give yourself the chance to calm your mind and come back to reality...where nothing is actually wrong.

But there's a reason why this is easier said than done. When you experience a high surge of anxiety, your body naturally thinks that you are in immediate danger and that something must be done about it right away. As this happens, your cortisol and adrenaline increase, causing several bodily reactions, and your awareness begins to look for what it is that might be causing you to be in danger.

As your symptoms increase as your physical body continues to respond, and as your awareness realizes that nothing outside of you is about to kill you, your awareness begins looking inward at your symptoms, in search of an explanation as to why you are feeling like you are about to die. Your racing heart suddenly becomes a heart attack, your dry mouth suddenly becomes you choking to death, and your tense muscles become some rare genetic disease that causes you to turn to dust and die. If you watch too many hospital dramas on television or spend too much time on WebMD, this may be a very familiar sequence for you.

Getting yourself to realize that your symptoms are simply a natural progression of stress and anxiety, and not a sign of imminent death can be challenging, especially if you have been allowing yourself to follow down the rabbit hole of fear for a particularly long time. Many anxiety sufferers find that no matter how many times they come out of a state of anxiety alive, this next time is definitely going to be the one time where they do not. As a result, they simply continue to spiral with every single new outburst, and this spiral works itself in as a natural response to the trigger of anxiety itself. In the end, anxiety becomes the very trigger that triggers their anxiety to get worse. Fun, right?

So this feels like a good time to talk about what the common symptoms of anxiety are, so you are able to point out what is completely normal, and what is cause for concern. Otherwise, a lack of awareness can make everything seem like a cause for concern, thus making it even harder to reasonably move through a bout of anxiety without going completely berserk. You need to know when to override the loud voice screaming, "Oh no, I'm having a heart attack!" with "No, that's just mild heart palpitations from anxiety." This perspective can also help you to convince yourself to calm down your anxiety in the moment. Then, in the rare occasion that something worse may actually be happening, you will have enough of an understanding of your anxiety that you will be able to easily decide that it is time for you to get serious medical help. You'll get a grip on your own symptoms so you can stop questioning whether or not it is time to call 9-1-1 every time your anxiety creeps in.

Common Symptoms Of Anxiety

Many people believe that anxiety is straightforward: when you have anxiety, you feel scared. Simple, right? Wrong. Anxiety comes with a whole slurry of physical, mental, and emotional symptoms. Moreover, some symptoms may impact you at some times but not others, which can make it challenging to decide whether that is a new anxiety symptom or a new cause for concern. Typically speaking, most new symptoms that spontaneously arise during a moment of high anxiety, such as a panic attack, are symptoms of your anxiety and nothing else. Obviously, this is not always the case—but more often than not, this is what's happening.

Symptoms of anxiety include things like:

- Feeling nervous, restless, or tense in your muscles and body
- Thinking that you are in danger or are doomed, feeling the urge to panic
- Heart palpitations, or increased heart rate
- Rapid breathing or hyperventilation
- Sweating
- Trembling
- Feeling very weak
- Sudden and sometimes intense fatigue
- Difficulty concentrating or thinking about anything beyond your present cause for concern
- Difficulty sleeping, sleeping too much, or sleeping too little
- Gastrointestinal problems including flatulence or symptoms mimicking irritable bowel syndrome
- Difficulty controlling your worrying thoughts
- The urge to avoid anything triggering your anxiety

- Frustration, irritability, or even angry outbursts
- Nausea, or in intense circumstances, vomiting
- Hopelessness and helplessness, feeling like no one—not even you—can calm yourself down
- Repetitive thoughts or intrusive thoughts
- Muscle twitches
- A tight chest which can create mild to moderate chest pains
- Dry mouth
- Feeling like you are not in control over the situation

All of these symptoms are common during moments of high anxiety or even panic attacks. Of course, some of these symptoms can mimic more serious situations, but in most cases, they are not. Instead, they are simply symptoms of your anxiety that you have yet to get under control. In many cases, simply identifying these symptoms and recognizing that they are natural to anxiety itself can help you relax and realize that what you are experiencing is natural and normal in a fearful situation, and it's not going to kill you.

Getting A Grip On Your Symptoms

Getting a grip on your anxiety means first getting a grip on your symptoms. If you are dealing with anxiety, getting to know your personal anxiety and your personal symptoms is the best way to really understand what you are going through and whether or not you should be concerned about new or different symptoms arising. We just went over a long list of symptoms in the section above, but they will not all pertain to you.

You can easily use your journal once again to track your own symptoms. This type of tracking will help you recognize the difference between experiencing something normal vs something abnormal for you. Understand that it is actually quite common for people to completely forget what their previous anxious experience was like and so when the next one pops up, they begin to believe that they are having new symptoms so it's time to ring the alarm—when, in reality, the symptoms they are having are ones they have had in the past. Having a log of your symptoms will not only show you what is normal for you but will also help bring ease to your mind if you find yourself forgetting what your typical symptoms are like and panicking over what you could initially convince yourself to be a whole new level of anxiety attack.

Once you have figured out the ways your body responds to anxious moments, decide to start being realistic with yourself about what you are going through. From now on, when you start having anxiety, give yourself permission for it to just be anxiety, not always automatically assuming that it's something else. In the moment, you can allow yourself to recognize what exactly is going on with your body and feel through it until it's over. The more that you give yourself this freedom to experience the physical response to anxiety without trying to blow it up into something bigger than it is, the less powerful anxiety feels because you realize that it is simply another harmless emotion. Yes, it may be uncomfortable, and it may make you feel like you are dying—but you know for a fact that you are not, and therefore, you do not need to heighten your anxiety with fears of your impending mortality.

Sometimes, making "friends" with your anxiety by getting to know it and fully understanding what triggers it and how it responds to triggers can make a world of difference. Knowing what your anxiety is like and how it behaves will not necessarily stop it from happening, but it will make it more predictable so that you no longer feel like you are being taken over by the overwhelming, unbearable symptoms. The more you can lean into your predictions and observations, the easier it is going to be for you to identify it in the future and ride it out.

When It May Be Something More

On the off chance that your anxiety may actually be turning into something more, if you have been a good little student and journaling your self-reflections, you should know. Instead of being sporadic and manageable, symptoms that are cause for true concern are more likely to be more intense to the point where you will not be able to deny them for what they are—they will produce intense discomfort that completely takes over your awareness. I say this not so that you can start fixating on your symptoms and blowing them up into something bigger than what they are, but so that you can differentiate between your anxiety symptoms and the much larger thing that you think they might be. Doctors say that anxiety rarely leads to something more serious like a heart attack, so it is safe for you to assume that your symptoms are generally benign.

If you tend to be an anxiety sufferer who believes that every little thing is going to be the death of you, you may feel more confident by finding a doctor who is aware of anxiety and compassionate towards those who suffer with it. This way, you can give them your log, and they can let you know what symptoms are normal, and they can track things with you. Sometimes, having a medically trained professional who can let you know that everything is okay and that you are okay is a powerful way to keep yourself from falling into the belief that you are doomed. This way, you have reassurance and validation that it really is just a tense muscle and not the onset of some deadly disease that decided to spontaneously increase to level 100 in a matter of three minutes. No, you are not one of the very unfortunate fictional patients on those hospital procedural shows, and you are not going to have the rarest of rare deaths known to man. You truly are not that special, so again, chill out, bro.

CHAPTER 28

DON'T BE A PAIN IN YOUR OWN...

DO you have a friend who seems to have issues with everything in their life constantly? Their friends are never treating them right, their partner is always a major problem, their job is always causing them stress, and they always seem to be down on their luck. No matter how much time passes between your conversations, you can almost always guarantee that the next time you talk, this person is going to have at least a half dozen new, life-shattering, major problems that always end in nothing more than them complaining about them. Maybe you have tried to pep them up, and they seem somewhat positive for a few minutes, but then before you know it, they slip back into complaining about something new, or find a way to poke holes in the positivity. Yeah, that person can be a real pain in the ass. Don't be that person.

After you have done the work of learning more positive coping strategies, and going down the path of being a more positive person in general so that you can release your anxiety and start feeling decent, it is important that you also do the work to maintain it. Falling back into your old patterns is easier than you might think, and believe it or not, it actually has psychological reasoning behind it, which means that it may not be so easy for you to escape this pattern. If you do not want to be a pain in your own ass, you need to find your way through these psychological patterns so that you do not immediately regress into your old behaviors and find yourself thinking that all of the progress you made was just bound to be temporary or was just in your head.

Why Do We Regress?

Psychology has shown us that we regress into old patterns because that is where we find comfort or familiarity in our lives. Our brains like to believe that they are highly efficient and that once they have learned to do something once, there should be no reason to have to learn how to do it again. To our brains, having to relearn something that we have already learned is redundant and inefficient, and since our brains are all about efficiency, they are not always a big fan of letting us override this natural tendency. When you do choose to override your natural tendencies, you are tapping into something known as "willpower," which is essentially you consciously willing yourself to experience change in your brain. Unfortunately, sometimes willpower alone is not strong enough for us to create lasting changes, which means that we have to work even harder to make those changes stick.

A big reason why we "relapse" into old habits or behaviors is because either we have not fully finished switching into our newer behaviors, or we have encountered triggers that we have not yet neutralized. When either of these scenarios is true, those neural pathways that have not yet been completely diminished are retriggered, and we find ourselves engaging in our old behaviors again.

For some habits we have had, we can never fully erase these neural pathways, so you will always be in a state of managing your habits and behaviors to ensure that you do not fall back into old patterns. For others, they eventually disappear over time, and after several years of not engaging in the old behavior any longer, those pathways collapse, and you no longer need to worry about engaging in the behavior anymore.

When it comes to something like anxiety, the former can often be the case, as you likely have anxiety pretty deeply wired into you and you likely have far more symptoms than even you realize. Furthermore, anxiety is an emotion that you will sometimes continue to encounter due to the nature of life, so unlike something such as nail biting which can be avoided entirely, feelings of anxiety cannot always be avoided entirely. While you may sometimes be able to completely eliminate a negative response or feeling in reaction to an anxiety-inducing trigger, don't be discouraged if you are not able to totally make an anxious response disappear. Just focus on managing your anxiety so you are in control of it instead of it being in control of you. That is still a win.

Make Discomfort Comfortable

You may be thinking "Discomfort by definition is uncomfortable. That's why they call it *dis*comfort, and not comfort. So how can you possibly make discomfort comfortable?" And that is a very valid question. You would not lie on a nail or roll around in a bed of spikes and call it comfortable, so how can you hide in your anxiety and trick yourself into believing that this experience is in any way comfortable? The truth is: it is not comfortable, you are just living inside of your comfort zone, which is an illusion that your mind has created for you so that you can feel safe in your environment.

For people who have existed with anxiety or overwhelm for a long period of time, those feelings can become very familiar. In order to help you exist there long-term without feeling like you are absolutely losing your ever-loving marbles, your brain begins to identify ways to cope, which ultimately starts with making this state feel "normal" to you so that you do not feel like you are on the verge of a mental breakdown. Your brain finding comfort and familiarity in this frazzled mental state means that even though you are out of control, your brain has normalized it to the point where you do not *feel quite* so out of control. This way, you can at least find some kind of comfort in this zone, even if you do not actively see that comfort when you are riding in the peaks of your worries and fears.

By making this feel normal for you, your brain turns anxiety into your comfort zone. So, when you find your way out of anxiety and overwhelm, suddenly, your brain thinks you are in danger because you are not being subjected to that familiar level of discomfort and stress. Ah, the cruel and unfortunate irony. As a result, you find yourself feeling subjected to a completely different type of stress—the type of stress that comes from not being familiar with your surroundings and your present experiences.

In order for you to overcome this stress, you need to be willing to find comfort *outside* of your comfort zone so that eventually the freedom from anxiety and overwhelm becomes your new comfort zone and your new normal. This way, your brain can actually get it right, and you do not find yourself being duped by your brain's attempt at protecting you by making you feel like being on the brink of a meltdown is in any way "normal."

What Can I Do To Prevent This?

Preventing yourself from falling back into old patterns requires you to ensure that you see your shifts all the way through, and to be prepared for unexpected triggers to be pulled along the way. Both of these are the most common reasons why people will "relapse" into old patterns, so getting yourself prepared by preventing these two situations is the best way that you can avoid falling back into your anxious behaviors that you are trying to free yourself from.

It is important that you are continually consciously working on instilling your new patterns and behaviors until they come automatically to you. Even then, you should consciously check in every so often and make sure that you are still following your newer and more productive patterns in place of your older, less productive ones. If you think that you no longer have to think about it, then you are ending the conscious part of the process far too soon. You need to stay consciously involved in following your new pattern until one day the conscious element of it falls away naturally, and you find yourself just doing it automatically.

This is not a process that you can think about or consciously decide on. It just happens one day. And eventually, one day, you look back and realize that at some point you no longer had to think about it, it just happened. Once you do realize that the new patterns are just coming to you automatically, make sure that every so often you do your best to think about your new process and ensure that you are still doing it in a way that serves your new and improved way of thinking so that you can prevent yourself from falling back into your old one, and leave that mess behind for good.

You also need to have a plan in place for how you are going to handle unexpected triggers. Typically, triggers will catch you off guard at various points throughout your life and sometimes they will send you back into outdated behaviors that you thought you gave up on a long time ago. A friend of mine was a smoker, and after four years of not smoking, she decided to buy a pack of cigarettes one day because something happened that made her feel that life had gotten too stressful for her. That same day, she smoked two cigarettes and not only did she feel super guilty, but she got super sick as well. Disappointed in herself, she threw the rest of the pack out and decided to get back on board with revisiting another coping method for stress that did not involve smoking. Fortunately, this happened quickly for her, and she was back on the wagon in no time. For some people, however, one unexpected trigger out of left field can send them down a deep spiral that can have them feeling like they need to start from ground zero with their healing all over again.

The best way to avoid an anxiety relapse around unexpected triggers is to decide ahead of time what you are going to do should you get caught by surprise. Maybe if you have an unexpected trigger, you will chew gum, meditate for three minutes, remove yourself from the situation momentarily, or begin using your journal again until you get through the hardest part of the trigger being pulled. If you can get past riding the wave of the emotion in that first initial window of time after it's triggered, you'll find that brief moment of pause is often enough to calm you back down to rational thought that allows you to choose a healthy response.

Regardless of what plan you make, allowing yourself to have a plan in place is going to ensure that you feel confident that should any trigger be pulled, you know how you are going to respond to prevent a full out fall back. Of course, these triggers are unexpected, so you also need to be patient with yourself if you find that you handle the experience worse than you thought. This does not mean that you are a total dud and that you have completely failed yourself and there is no hope for you ever getting over your anxiety. Instead, it simply means that you have found a neural pathway that was not overwritten yet, therefore your brain has not had the chance to rewire that trigger yet. Go through all of the same steps that you did before, choose a new response, and watch as your anxiety melts away and you begin to feel far more in control and successful with your new coping method.

What If I Catch Myself Doing It?

If you do catch yourself slipping back into old behaviors, acknowledge it, and then consider stepping back into practice with some ACT therapy steps. Accepting that you have slipped backward and that you are engaging in old behaviors is the best way to make sure that you do not hold on to any unnecessary shame around this slip-up, which could further hold you back. Once you have accepted that you made an uh-oh, you can begin going back to square one and starting the process of ACT all over again.

You want to start right from the very beginning of identifying your trigger, understanding why you slipped up, and tracking your progress forward as you use your coping methods to unscrew yourself. This may feel like a total kick in the behind because you have to start from square one, but understand that your brain already has new neural pathways laid out that will help you engage in the new behavior once again. This time, you are not starting from ground zero and completely rewiring everything—you are just getting yourself back on track. You will likely find that it is not as hard as you think to make this happen, so just keep yourself motivated by reminding yourself of your past success, and keep working forward. No matter what, you are not a total screw up, and your slip-ups are not a sign of something major being wrong with you. You are just a human with a normal functioning brain that is behaving in a way that is driving you crazy, and you happen to have the courage to try to trick it into working to your advantage. No big deal, right?

CONCLUSION

Anxiety can be a real piece of work. If you have been dealing with it for a while, chances are that you have seen it painted in many different ugly colors—from clutching your chest, begging your body not to give up on you as you relive something mortifying that you said three weeks ago, to biting your nails down to the knuckle in anticipation of an upcoming meeting, to physically and mentally freezing in a moment of high pressure—anxiety is almost never pretty.

And you likely know from personal experience that it's possible to have problematic anxiety from time to time without necessarily having a diagnosable mental illness. When life gets overwhelming, something unexpected throws more timber into your fire, or you find that you are not taking great care of yourself at a particular moment, your body and mind can respond to stress a little more dramatically. Either way, getting your nervous breaks under control so that you can start feeling more at peace in your life is necessary if you want to get back to enjoying a higher quality of life overall, and hopefully, that has come to feel more possible with the help of this book.

Remember Jason from the beginning of the book? Jason has completely turned his life around since getting a handle on his anxiety.

He broke up with Lindsey...and survived. He always knew their relationship wasn't healthy, but he finally got tired of allowing the negative cycle to continue, so as difficult as it was, he took control and accountability, sat down with Lindsey, explained to her why the relationship wasn't working for him, and broke it off for good. After he did it, he realized it wasn't as bad as he thought it was going to be, and he realized that he can be single without feeling alone.

The extra free time gave him plenty of nights to himself for journaling and getting to know himself on a deeper level. After some self-reflection, Jason remembered that when he was younger, he saw his older sister get booed off stage at a school play, and ever since then, he hated the idea of speaking in front of people. He realized he was borrowing this negative experience as his own, and his self-reflection also reminded him that he used to be a real jokester and class clown before that point. So he started doing open mic nights at comedy clubs to tap back in to his childhood gift and passion, and he's quickly becoming a bit of a local celebrity.

This newfound confidence has bled over into his work, and he got a promotion. As for his social life, he realized that the people he was so afraid of judging him, were actually afraid that he would judge them, so he no longer had a reason to skip out on those happy hour socials with his coworkers. Now, they've become pretty close and whenever things get overwhelming for him, his new work buddies have proven to be a great support system to help calm him down and put things into perspective.

He got rid of his therapy cat. Ever since he started a daily pain diary and started working through his triggers, he doesn't feel like he needs the cat anymore.

He got rid of the ergonomic chair. With his life on a great new path, he didn't want the memory of the sadistic cat to give him the shakes every time he looked at that chair. He tried to sell it on craigslist, but too many people complained about cat scratches, so he just put it on the curb and let the garbageman pick it up.

And Lindsey? After desperately applying and interviewing for over 50 jobs at other marketing agencies, she realized that she can still be okay if things don't go exactly her way, and if she's open to different possibilities, something even better than her original plan can show up. That possibility showed up by way of a man she met in line at Starbucks who offered her a high level job at his successful startup after seeing how meticulously she prepared her coffee. She's able to use her attention to detail for good, without being high strung and inflexible.

If Jason and Lindsey can turn things around, you can too.

You may feel like your anxiety is a total drag and that you

are never going to be able to experience a life without it—and if you keep upholding that story, then I don't think I have to tell you that it will continue to be true. However, if you choose to take different actions, you can rewrite your story and start empowering yourself to rewire your brain so that it actually functions in your favor. No matter how deep in the hole you may feel, you can always make change by getting committed to your well-being and staying focused on putting new practices into place.

The key here is that you need to stay focused on your growth and progress, and avoid falling into traps that may hold you back. Remember, your brain is wired to yank you back into a false comfort zone, so you need to learn to be stronger than your brain. The more willing you are to stay on top of things and keep yourself focused on your growth, the more successful your growth will be overall, which will keep you continually moving forward effectively. You *need* to stay on top of things, though, and avoid getting complacent. If you do get complacent and start throwing your new habits out the window, then you will only have yourself to blame for once again succumbing to all of the crazy triggers that riddle you with anxiety.

After you put this book down, I really urge you to...get another one of my books...but also dig into your journal and start tracking your anxiety and getting a clear picture of what is and is not working for you. Keeping this book handy near your journal may even be helpful in getting you where you need to go by giving you the opportunity to flip back through the pages and remind yourself about the practices that you have learned and maybe forgotten about. Reminding yourself of these practices will make it easier for you to actually use them and make a freaking difference in your life already!

So I leave you with one last encouraging word. You, my friend, are totally capable of kicking anxiety's ass right out your door. There is absolutely no reason why you cannot whip your brain back into shape and stop being yanked around by anxiety, so do not, for one minute, think that you do not totally have this thing under control. If you are ready to get into action and put in the work to make a difference in your life, then know that you can totally do just that. You are stronger than your fears. You are stronger than your worries. You are stronger than your anxiety. And you are in control of your mind. So get out there, get to work, put these practices in action, and for Pete's sake, *chill out, bro!*

If you enjoyed this book in any way, please leave a review on Amazon, letting us know why you loved this book. And be sure to be on the lookout for other ebooks, paperback books and audiobooks by yours truly, Reese Owen, on Amazon and Audible.

LIKE WHAT YOU JUST READ? PLEASE LEAVE A REVIEW ON AMAZON

★ ★ ★ ★ ★

If you enjoyed this book and feel empowered to take control over your life, I ask that you leave a review on Amazon.

Your feedback is greatly appreciated. Hearing your opinion and understanding how my (hopefully) inspiring experiences and understandings may help you improve your own life is valuable in helping me to continue producing great content to support you in living your best life.

Plus, it makes me smile inside to see I'm able to have a positive effect on someone else's life with my antics.

Thanks a million,

-Reese

ME, AGAIN...

Thanks a bunch for getting this book!

Sad that it's over?

Turn that frown upside down. If you don't want the fun to end, below are all the ebooks, paperback books, and audiobooks I have available on Amazon and Audible.

B*TCH DON'T KILL MY VIBE:

HOW TO STOP WORRYING, END NEGATIVE THINKING, CULTIVATE POSITIVE THOUGHTS, AND START LIVING YOUR BEST LIFE

JUST DO THE DAMN THING:

HOW TO SIT YOUR @SS DOWN LONG ENOUGH TO EXERT WILLPOWER, DEVELOP SELF DISCIPLINE, STOP PROCRASTINATING, INCREASE PRODUCTIVITY, AND GET SH!T DONE

MAKE YOUR BRAIN YOUR B*TCH:

MENTAL TOUGHNESS SECRETS TO REWIRE YOUR MINDSET TO BE RESILIENT AND RELENTLESS, HAVE SELF CONFIDENCE IN EVERYTHING YOU DO, AND BECOME THE BADASS YOU TRULY ARE

CPSIA information can be obtained
at www.ICGtesting.com
Printed in the USA
LVHW041253060322
712740LV00008B/394

9 781951 238162